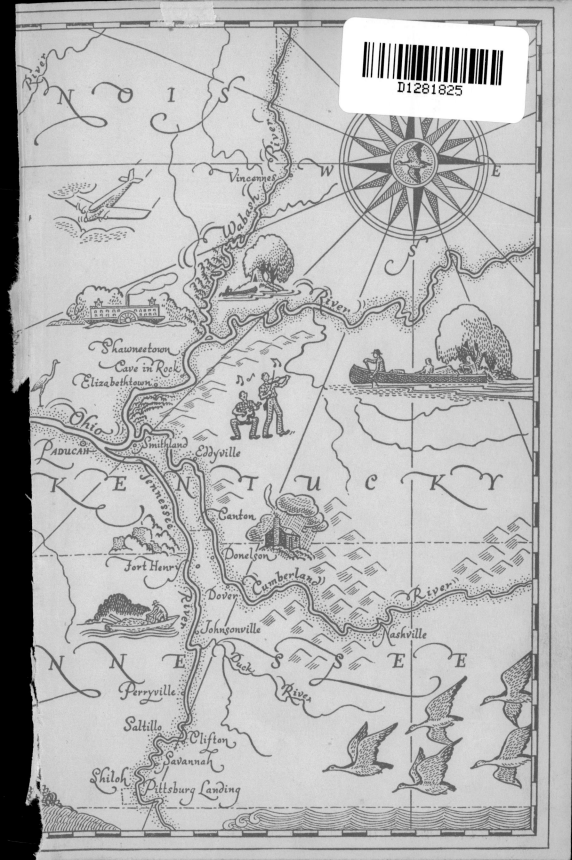

# WHERE THE RIVERS MEET

BY

## WARD DORRANCE

≈≈≈

*Keep silence before me, oh islands.*
*Let the people renew their strength.*
ISAIAH XLI

≈≈≈

*New York*
CHARLES SCRIBNER'S SONS
*1939*

*To*

JERRY BURKE

# Contents

~~~~~~~~~~~~~~~~~~~~~~~~~~~~~~

# I

## "ALSO, IN VIRGINIA..."

# "Also, in Virginia..."

WHEN DAVID LLOYD-GEORGE came to Saint Louis he was met by a delegation of prominent citizens. They had worn top hats so frequently that they could get in and out an automobile without knocking them off. They looked right well in the photograph. If Mr. Lloyd-George had asked what *alum co am* or *anacon cop* had "done" the day before, they could have answered in chorus. If he had desired statistics for the port of Saint Louis, they'd have sounded off as one man. But they were nigh flabbergasted when he wanted to be shown the confluence of the Missouri and the Mississippi. Seems none of our boys had ever been near the place. It's a good stretch north of town, and a man would get his spats benastied up there in the gumbo of the bottoms. Worse, there would be no advantage in being seen there.

Reception committees are chosen from the ranks of men who have got the most money out of a country. They regard themselves as its final achievement; the leaf and ripe fruit of a process which no longer needs to be studied.

But this is the truth about committee members; if it were not for the confluence of the rivers they would be wearing top hats elsewhere; or, more probably still, they would be grubbing turnips (with stocking caps for their only headgear) in Ireland or in Germany.

A man standing on the bank where the Missouri meets the Mississippi knows that he is looking at a hub of American history. He remembers how on the one hand water descends from the portages to Canada; how on the other a flood comes down from the Yellowstone and the Platte —the highway, before overland trails, into the last West. He will recall that these streams, joined, move on the South; that shortly there will be flushed into them the Ohio, swollen with the Youghiogheny, the Monongahela, the Kanawha, the Wabash, the Cumberland, and the Tennessee. He will remind himself that this convergence of eastern rivers guided incoming tides of settlers to the Mississippi; that, once arrived at the Mississippi, their impetus was not checked, because they found the Missouri a natural extension of the Ohio route.

At least the man will know these things if he has "discovered" the South and West; if he has had enough intelligence to piece out his own story of America. Very likely he heard nothing about it in schools. When I first held a text in my hands, except for the time Great-aunt Pamela Shelley went to England, no member of my family had been north of the line in a hundred years. New England is therefore not my country, as the text said; it is the country of New Englanders. It is one of a confederation of sections that brought forth Calamity Jane and Sitting Bull as well as Mr. Longfellow. But the text was given over almost entirely to New England. It bundled *La Nouvelle France* into a paragraph. It treated the Spanish occupation as an unconfirmed rumor. It did not say that the Latins in moving from Canada to the Gulf, from Florida to the Mississippi, had broken trails that resembled paths of stars. It told us that the French and Spanish had lost their hold in North America, but it did not tell us why. It admitted that Boone killed a bear in Kentucky, but it did not explain his exit from the Piedmont; or say why he was there in the first place; or tell what happened after he left. It gave what sounded like one man's hunting expedition. When we had finished the history of New England and the Middle Atlantic States we were given only one clue to the rest—the tail end of a chapter beginning: "Also, in Virginia . . ."

A second text should have taken up the story there. It should have said that for a hundred and fifty years settlement on the east coast was hemmed by a mountain wall from Alabama to Maine; that when land was taken up in the plain, and the new man and the poor man began to find no place, settlers moved towards the mountains. Following the Susquehanna, the Potomac, the James and the Roanoke they came to the "fall line." From here they went afoot. But in tracing back rivers they had discovered the passes. If this had not happened the United States, as Europeans predicted, would have remained a seacoast nation.

## *Where the Rivers Meet*

On trails cut out by game and Indians the settlers got
over the first hills and found the parallel valleys, the
troughs of the Appalachian range. Here most of them
remained until after the French and Indian War. This
sojourn was of capital importance for the future nation.
Back on the coastal plain a man was not only, in effect,
still a European; he was a Pennsylvanian or a Carolinian.
He felt himself to be different and he was different. Here
in the valleys the line of movement was north-south. English, Scotch-Irish, Dutch and Huguenot met and blended,
forming for the first time a true American type. The settler who resulted from this mingling, when he had lived
a while in the solitude of woods and in the real democracy
of the frontier village, became for the conservative dwellers of the coast, as well as for the Indians, a terrible man.
Daniel Boone took his gun and his dog and left the Legis-
lature of Virginia because he was plumb bored. Andrew
Jackson stayed.

The Crown Proclamation of 1763 would have held the
frontiersman to territory drained by seaboard river sources.
But the frontiersman felt that he, not the British, had won
the French and Indian War. Now he wanted the fruit
of his trouble—the land of the Ohio valley. He was no
longer an easy man to discipline. He did not respect the
Proclamation. He found that the headwaters of the rivers
he had followed from the coast interlocked with those of
the Ohio and the Tennessee. From the Susquehanna, the
Juniata and the Potomac he could get into the Youghiogheny, into the Monongahela. From the James and the

6

Roanoke he could reach the New, the Greenbriar, the Kanawha, and the Holston. This discovery was as important for American history as the Revolution itself. Once a boat was launched on the upper Ohio the whole country out to the great falls of the Missouri already belonged to us.

Pioneers followed rivers because rivers offered them the line of least resistance, and because rivers served their economic need. In the flat boats and barges that succeeded the canoe of the Indian trade they swept downstream, alternately firing guns and singing hymns. In this new land there were no natural barriers. There was water. There was wood. There was salt. There was elbow room. There were venison and good duck and no game wardens. Men went hog wild. The bigness of the West had got into their bones.

At the Mississippi there was an attempt to halt them. New England and the Middle Atlantic States were willing to accept Jay's treaty closing the lower river. They opposed the Louisiana Purchase, pointing out that the north-south course of the Mississippi would divert western interests to the South. But the frontiersman had his way once more. He threatened to march against the Spanish—until the Mississippi was opened to him. He talked of joining with the British of Canada—and Louisiana was bought for him. Without the Purchase the story of Louisiana would have been that of Texas and California. It would have been a matter of time. There were already Americans in the villages and back country of the west

7

bank of the Mississippi from New Madrid to Saint Louis. There were Americans on the Saint François River and the White; on the Maramec, on the Gasconade and the Osage. It was inevitable that they should be there. "A drainage system forms an unbroken whole. The common destination of tributary streams makes it as easy to cross as to follow the structural axis of the basin." The Missouri was there stretching out to the West. It led directly into the northern fur fields. It spanned the base of the Rockies with its headwaters. Along its shores outpost displaced outpost as the starting point to Oregon and Santa Fé.

In school we should have been told something of this. The story of the rivers was our story. My brother and I would have seen in it almost a family history. Whether on the Santee in 1718, the Coosa in 1815, the Cumberland in 1830, or the Missouri in 1870, our men had always had a river to live on. There had been flour- and sawmills to build; landings and ferries. There had been fish to catch, floods to fight, water to listen to and watch. Our own first sight of the out-of-doors was a bend in the Missouri. The first tales we heard concerned the river. Indians had made signal fires on the bluffs we climbed. A skeleton in Spanish uniform had been dug out of a mound on the bank. French trappers, coming down from the Yellowstone, had slept in a cave we knew. Lewis and Clark had sent a man to explore the creek we swam in. There one day when Cousin Leo was fishing, he looked over the edge of his boat and saw a stone that had fallen from the cliff into the water. "Had buffalo painted on it, seemed like," said Cousin Leo, "and deer. Or maybe elk. A man couldn't tell." At night, under the patchwork quilt, I would tell my brother the tale of Uncle Jim: how he used to drive an express wagon across on the ice when he was a boy, before the Missouri was bridged; how late one afternoon he was "bewildered" in a fog on the river.

A quarter of a mile from shore mist closed about him, so that he lost both banks and his feel of the straight line in between. "Better wheel about," he thought. "Better go straight back." He turned his team, but in his excitement he forgot to watch the wheels. He was not sure they had made a complete revolution. He shut his eyes, trying to recall the swing of his body on the box. He got down to look for tracks, but there were none on the ice. He stood for an instant to still his panic, hoping to sight a landmark. Fog was wadded thick as high as his belt. It rose to the Clydesdales' bellies, hiding their legs. It blotted the lower half of the wheels that were high and sunken at the hub. Above that level it thinned, and here and there a whisp of it twirled as if it were coming out of a chimney. But a man could not see twenty feet. Even so, Uncle Jim decided, he'd better keep moving. It was ice, not faith, that was holding him up. The horses weighed 1200 pounds apiece. He didn't know about the van. If they stayed long in one place a line of cleavage might shoot about them, quickly, as cracks dart over a freezing pitcher. Then they would be on a floating cake that would tilt. Probably the van would go down first. It would pull

9

the horses after it. Their hooves would be in his face.
They would kick him to death before he could drown.
Then the cake would settle back in place, covered with
brown water and a little blood. He started out. He would
have liked to lay his whip out over the horses, to see them
lunge and settle in a gallop. But horses do not run on the
ice in a fog. He had to beat down his fear, to cram it in
small space though it ate at him the more sharply for
being cramped. It was over an hour before he saw lights.
They were round and dim, making no brightness beyond
their globes. Uncle Jim had not crossed the river. He was
two miles downstream, on the bank he had left. If ladies
were around he always allowed you could have knocked
him down with a feather. To us he said: "Boys, in another minute you'd have had to clean me!"

In this way there was an unbroken line between us and
the Indians: the Osages, the Sauks and Foxes that built
the signal fires. Rivers wound in and out their tribal history and in and out of ours. For us, when we were boys,
the rivers still provided sights that had been common to
Indian boys: a snake twitching rattles from under the
prickly pear of a ledge; catfish four feet long, carried on
poles between men's shoulders; geese in a "v" following
the Missouri up there as if the Missouri were straight.
We saw deer, killed on the Osage, hanging by their feet;
we touched the convolute edge of the gash that split their
belly. We saw wolf pups, caught in the islands, displayed
in windows like white rabbits at Easter. And we found a
drowned man. His head had nudged a place in the sand

where the water kept sucking him out and shoving him in. His flesh gave under the hook. "You kids go tell them ladies they have to stand back," the deputy had said. "Hit ain't only that he stinks. When a drownded man swells up he swells all over, if you git what I mean."

My brother and I were not the only boys who played by the river. We were two of a great number. Every one had a cousin who owned a houseboat; an uncle who'd caught a ninety-pound cat; or a father who'd been lost in the duck season, pulled under by his heavy boots. Brother and I had a little edge on the rest because our cousin had an eye put out during a dove shoot on the Osage. But we in turn deferred to the boy whose grandfather had been captain of the *Western Star* (looted and sunk by the Yankees at Malta Bend). Down to our generation our families every one had been affected by the river.

Before we were grown the scene began to change. I date it from the morning Mother called me from the yard to see a horseless carriage. It was scarlet and built like a buggy. It had a chain drive that went limp and fell off now and then. It dropped in the road with a *plup!* of dust same as when one of us threw away a snake, after we'd whip-cracked his head off. We saw more and more horseless carriages after that. Uncle Will stopped taking the family to the river in a wagon. Grandpa never drove the old fringed surrey any more. Cars became common. Even we got one. Then they began to pave the roads and we could go anywhere quick. We thought nothing of driving home from college for a dance, and back to class first thing in the morning. We had to cross the Missouri on Highway 63, of course. But there was always traffic, and a sign which said: *No Parking on the Bridge.* If we saw the river at all it was out of the corner of an eye. We'd got pretty far from the Indians.

Yet the idea of rivers stayed in my mind—active, but furtive, like a rat behind a row of barrels. In the midst of rooms full of people, a spring morning would come back to me. I would be standing on a bank where columbine grew high. Its colored bells struck my cheek as I thrust the stems aside. I moved through them out to the end of a sand point. The width of the Missouri sparkled before me. The even swell of midstream reached the shore. It sent a lather between my toes. The wind found out my armpit, my ribs and navel. It was passionate and light. It carried out the slack of my trouser legs and shirt. My thigh was molded down to my knee as if the pants were wet.

Such memories would move into my consciousness as trout dart at a hook. And they would come at the very moment when I was talking to a dowager in a red evening gown. I could resolve to concentrate on her bulldog cheeks; on the babies' buttocks of her breasts lying nude in the shell of her bodice. But when she tapped me with her fan I jumped.

While the horseless carriage had been growing up, so had I. It had been necessary to enter an organization called society. That meant paying my taxes and keeping the weeds out of my lawn. It meant discussing the probable absorption of Yugoslavia with the dowager, who interrupted herself to say, oh, good *evening,* Colonel Harrington. It meant remaining until two in the morning with a crowd of people whose conversation, from a little distance, sounded like a dog show. It meant buying a lot of Roquefort and having the gang to *my* house.

When I balked, my friends let me know that they considered my case elementary. I was an escapist. When I pointed out that every man not already insane is an escapist, they hinted at some more fundamental eccentricity. When I declared that the automobile, the ticker tape and cocktail parties are instruments of the grossest kind of escapism, they said, My God, you're one of *those!* When I pointed out that society does not mean urban society alone; that I might be a farmer or a rancher or an Indian on a reservation and still fall within the pale, they moved off to get another drink and to get back down to Yugoslavia. I let them go. Not one of them had sense enough to keep his shadow from falling across a bass hole, anyway.

Yet when I announced that I was going away to live on the rivers for a while, they gathered around again. They looked at the circle I had drawn on the map. They listened while I explained that within the circle the Osage and the Gasconade flow into the Missouri; the Missouri and the Illinois into the Mississippi; the Wabash, the Cumberland and the Tennessee into the Ohio; and the Ohio into the Mississippi. They looked up when I said that this meeting of rivers had served as a kind of cockpit for our history.

I told them I was going to "put in" at a village on the Osage. Out of that river I should enter the Missouri, and go down the Missouri to the Mississippi. I should go up the Mississippi into the Illinois, and when I had seen something of the Illinois I should descend to the Mississippi again, and follow it to the mouth of the Ohio. Then I should ascend in turn the Ohio, the Tennessee, the Cumberland and the Wabash.

How was I going to travel? In an eighteen-foot canoe; square-sterned to take a little motor; equipped with air chambers to steady me in rough water. It would have the buoyancy of the canoe with the stability of a boat. It would be called *Ni-sho-dse*, Muddy Water, the Osage Indian name for the Missouri River.

Where should I sleep? In an umbrella tent. But snakes? And mosquitoes? The tent would have net doors and a sewn-in floor. Did I know that the Mississippi could toss up water ten feet high in storms? That when it is apparently calm it suddenly opens whirlpools fifty feet across? Wasn't I afraid? Was it certain that I could manage the boat alone? Man by man they got me aside. Twenty-five or thirty of them thought they had better go with me. They said that with a little notice they could get their affairs in order. Their eyes glittered.

In the end, of course, I could take only two. But it was good to see so many faces glow. I felt that the men were moved by something deep in the past they had forgot. In this one, as he spoke, it was Grandfather Faircloth leaving Virginia again. In that one a Mountjoy or a Duke was walking the buffalo trail from Carolina. They were feeling their way to the portages of the Ohio. They were hearing the river slap at the bank with the sound that horses make when they trot in dust. They were watching reflections of stars that remain in place though they move on a fold of water. It was the old men working in their grandsons. They had got up their stock from out of the mountain. They had some side meat and a bag of meal. They were letting out their legs, heading west again; out to crests where a man can see the valleys shine.

## II

## RIVER OF THE GREAT OSAGES

# River of the Great Osages

O UR AMERICAN STREAMS, for the most part, were named by pioneers of our own blood, men content with brief identification. A little later they would have labelled rivers as we indicate highways: the Cumberland Pike has given its ducal name for the numeral 40.

Now and then they followed the Indian—so that the *Illinois*, the *Atchafalaya*, the *Kaskaskia*, roll their thunder yet. And here and there (but not docilely) they accepted the French—the *Marais des Cygnes* still lays its gamey smell about the map.

But these were generally great rivers already known. The small streams yet to be named were dismissed—impatiently, it would seem—as Deer or Panther Creek. And the matter rested there. It was not important if there were several of each in a given state.

Yet to the man who knows the stream its name cannot be vulgar. By banks of rivers good things happen. The water itself establishes an identity. It words its own clause in our experience. One morning at sunrise in a field I was galloping into the light and could not see. Blunt heads of insects hit my boot, and the cones of black-eyed-susan. I was not trying to watch ahead. I was wholly with the rhythm and the swish of hay. Suddenly the horse leaped, not breaking the count of his gallop. I gasped, and as the black mane stung like sand across my mouth, looked down. I saw—I being then at that moment on a horse in air—a bright blade of water. "Duck Creek," said the groom who rode behind me. . . . It is not distinguished, but it is name enough for me. At the sound of it I am once more on a horse superb of mane and tail. Between my thighs I feel the effort of his back as he leaps from earth, sundering mist towards a sun red and swollen over the salt-white peaks.

On the other hand the names of some streams, like the names of some men, seem born to fame. Like a line of great verse they lay about them with a whip. *The Red River of the North, the Black Warrior of Alabama, La Rivière des Grands Osages.*

When in the seventeenth century Father Marquette recorded their name, the Osages had claimed already for a hundred years the land that rolls, richly wooded, from the bluffs of the Missouri to the swamps of the Arkansas. In the ritual of their religion they are divided into groups referring to Sky, Dry Land and Water. It was the name of the latter, the *Wa-zhá-zhe,* which the French retained for the whole nation, and which they pronounced *Osage.* The name is old, so old that modern tribesmen find its meaning dim. But it has to do with running water.

20

# River of the Great Osages

This people came to earth from stars. Their wanderings brought them to a bank from which they saw a man who stood hip-deep in water churning over rock. And their leader faced them, saying: "Yonder stands *Wa-zhá-zhe.* He has made of the moving water of earth his body [his patron, his life-symbol]." Then over the tumble of rapids, a voice: "Make of me your bodies and your little ones shall be difficult to be overtaken by death. They shall enable themselves to see great age. They shall also come to the days which are beautiful." Therefore the brown tribe, silent beyond the foam, took a name which showed that they so-called had given themselves to the mid-rushing water.

Other phenomena of geography and geology are static, or seem to be by the standard of time forced upon us. But a stream does something. It moves.

It is good to know the chemistry of the crust of stars; to note migration of the flounder's eye; to peel off alternate record of drought and flood from the wet nipples of cavern floors. But we note these things when they are through with action.

We can see the stream move. It is less impersonal than the twirl and pull of wind. We can watch it shaking the chinquapin stems, dissolving clods, breaking the moonlight into flakes. Through its clarity that seems to magnify we can see the sun-fish fanning her nest, the whitening bone of a heron's leg, the backward running of the crayfish. We can peer over the moist nose of a boat as level and leisurely bass move in and out of caves.

21

The ancient Osage, squatting on the bank, thrust his toes to the leaf-mold and knew earth. His priest sang: "Acts of touching the earth are divine."

He watched the nervous tail of flame and knew fire. With it he made charcoal of redbud wood. Before battle the priest smeared it on his face. It symbolized the impartial flame; neither fire nor warrior gives or asks for quarter.

He felt the movement of the wind over the hide of his back, like the brush of fur, and he knew air. His priest sang: "The cedar at the edge of the cliff, standing with wrinkled ankles in the four paths of the wind, sends out a *gab-thon* [a wind-riding fragrance]."

Now he heard *Wa-zhá-zhe* and knew water. And of the manifestations of Spirit about him he preferred that of running water. It was most potent. It had the biggest medicine. He took for his life symbol the river-having-four-bends. The stream, in his Genesis, says: "Little children who make of the cavity of my bed their bodies shall live to see great age. Their neck shall wrinkle, the thews of their inner thighs shall loosen, their toes shall fold over with great age."

Now, in June, in the month which the priest called the month of the rutting of the buffalo bull, the big-animal-that-stands-firmly-upon-earth, we too come to the River of the Great Osages. We are less modest than they. In making our bodies of the stream's hollow bed we ask more than age. We would make the spirit of the water to play over us slender and multiple, as in a fountain. We want cancellation of Time. . . .

Du Tisne and Pierre Chouteau and Pike and Washington Irving knew the Osages, and saw them here in their old home. But for more than a century now they are banned from their river, from the hills which they likened to the breasts of young turkeys. They were driven to Kansas, to flat Oklahoma, to prairies (little did Andrew Jackson dream!) greasy with rich oil. It is sixty years odd since they returned of summer nights to wail by the burial grounds; since they came back to the upper forks of the river, to the meeting of the Little Osage and the *Marais des Cygnes,* to *Mi-xa-çka u-tsi,* the spot-abounding-in-wild-swans. . . . As for the buffalo, the last was killed in 1840—he snorted and dropped in the tall-grass islands of the River Saint François.

Then for a while was peace. Into the valleys Southerners came, trailing with ferns that caught in the hubs the names Carolina, Kentucky. And tow-headed Germans came. They opened the loam and saw it was fat. They said to homesick wives: "Warum brüllst du? Alles ist hier so grün und schön!" . . . So green and lovely. . . .

Came a day when the first steamboat rounded the bend. If local legend is true it was watched by men who had climbed trees with their guns, thinking a giant "painter" was on its way. After that first came others, bearing fine names: the *Lightfoot,* the *Wave,* the *Alliance,* the *Allegheny Mail.* And they brought freight for points throughout the land as far as northwest Arkansas. Men who saw

23

it later said: "Child, it was a sight in this world!"

And then was war. Old folks say that gunboats moved up the Osage, bigger than buffalo but not unlike them swimming. These boats belonged to Northerners or, if one follows one's grandmother, to Republicans. They came sweeping the banks with guns, holding the land to a flag that now perforce is mine but once was not. . . . Here was trouble aplenty and here was a wildcat in every tree. In this border state there was no set battle to leave an issue standing cleanly, like a chimney of the fired house. There was rather a constant harrowing after the manner of "feudin' " rather than that of war. Water was knocked bodily from the shallow fords by hooves. Riders thundered to village streets with foam and sudden news. The smoke of burning homes went up over the oak wood, and the man of the house died without saying where he had hid his money. Cross-road mills gave up their smell of grain to stink of charred wood: the rat ran from his hole in the board, and after him the cat, both singed. Bushes parted; a single gun spoke; and the bushes mingled. Neighbor was victim of neighbor. The county bully had his day. . . .

Now the frontier is gone and strife is gone. The nation is said to be one and is middle-aged and has a paunch and the market is pretty steady these days. Where we launch our canoe there is no Indian, no buffalo, neither any gunboat whatsoever. A little county seat made to fit the hills, under the silver egg of its courthouse dome. Once it was a trading post. By its site went Pike, sailing to the West with Zebulon his name for a bowsprit. It was here at about this point that he saw how his sails would henceforth be useless; here that he cut down his mast and slipped it overboard. Here he left behind him the ways of the East. Here he looked out consenting to take the new land on its own terms—he the laconic; he who records: "Killed nine deer" when he is climbing the River of the Great Osages, fighting his way to its meeting with the River of the Marsh of Swans, heading for the Arkansas, for the desert beyond where his tongue will be swollen and he cannot cry out when he sees, as the Indians told him he would see, flashing from one hundred thousand brittle facets, The Mountains That Glitter.

We strip back the burlap and grass from the sides of our craft. That grass is grass that grew in the State of Maine, perhaps by the sea at Saturday Cove or Kennebunkport, names exotic to us as Tomsk or Mauna Loa. America is huge.

To reach the bank we must thread a crowd of natives who have come in cars, on bicycles and afoot, who have sent back children for more of their elders. They squat on their hunkers, unhurried, and talk. They tell of days before railroad and truck, when all freight for this country of the Osage came by steamboat from the Missouri. They are old. They were "raised on this water." They are not glutted with diversions. They live uncomplaining the time between news. They know how to make a pleasure last.

Their marvel now is the exquisite boat. They crowd around it, leaning far out to run their fingers over it; wading into the shallows to touch its intricate ribs; pushing down the nose to see it bounce back; observing that "they kain't no water git into hit nohow."

Says one: "Man, hit's worth a meal of victuals to look at a boat like that." Let it be recorded here for the manufacturers. One doubts if, in a world where men must eat, they have had better tribute.

And one adds who has just come up: "Why . . . hell, boys: that boat's out of a *catalogue!*" He thinks it may even have come from Montgomery Ward's. A thing like that'd fetch close to forty dollars. . . . I laugh, but I do not agree. Of the things our bills, our worn coins can buy, a boat has the least of the chain store about it. Whether a president's yacht or my canoe, it is not number three-seventy-eight of the day's production. It is fitted together individually. It smacks gratefully of "craft." It has behind it the workman who wears an apron; who walks in shavings shoe-mouth deep; who lifts his wood and his square to find no light between.

Why do men refuse themselves, once in their lives at least, the joy of launching a new boat? Of the sensations possible to flesh, why miss the hand's grip on the stern as the prow first touches water, sending out tremors? It is like touching a kite string, taut and hard. It is like the first contact of anything rare and until now forbidden. . . .

A shove of the paddle turns us to the current. We are

sucked from the shoaling-water into wind, into the wide light. We see the village in its crook of the stream as fishermen see it at sundown, running in for home. There is charm in the contrast of its humped domesticity with the stride of the river in its bend. The Osage, swollen in spring, is ready yet to take a war party anywhere it wants to go.

It sweeps us off beneath its ceiling of silence, into its picture framed in silence where I am, in this hour of setting out, far from taking to myself the holy calm. Rather I am tense, like a tilted hawk—in motion slow, but making full use of the eye in its socket, of the ear in the side of the head. I am off on the track of rain, of springs, of secret water from the clean places of the earth, water that goes with the strut of nigger camp singers (nipples erect with conviction): *"La-a-awd, Ah buckled on mah shoes and Ah stawted!"* Here where there is no sound but wind, but the bowstring hum of water, I am like the little man with derby, with walking stick and boutonnière, who is swept by accident into a parade. He bobs upon the surface of excitement. Drums lay hold of his legs and flex his knees. The elephants walk on his fallen hat. A camel munches his boutonnière. The calliope makes him hollow and fills him with sound, as a hydrant floods an empty hose making it writhe in the grass till its kinks are gone.

Only, I cannot march or twirl a baton. I must sit, my excitement compressed, in my pod of green canvas. Here where it was made to be, the canoe declares itself. Until today it was I who cared for it. Now it takes charge. I

27

see from and feel through it. Its nose rises and falls,
turning from side to side, as if it were gently refusing
something it does not want. It splits a way for the sleek
flanks, for the body which was the Indian's contribution
to the history of transportation, for the body to which
nothing can be added and nothing taken away. It is as
inevitable as the line of leaves. It is the lowest common
denominator of a series of possible forms. It is lovely and
useful, like the belly of a 'cello, the foot of a running
hound. It serves and pleases all. Two men, however different, see it each, as it were, with an eye of a same skull.

The Indian, leaving to put on pants in the reservations,
looked over his shoulder and gave us this. He condensed
his race into an epigram. He made orderly and single his
song, his hunt, his tumult of drums, the mane of his horse.
And he added, to make sure we should not misunderstand,
the quivering of a young doe, she being arrow-struck.

When a man, with the warmth of his mattress still upon
him, steps from his windless room into a boat, there are
moments of painfully tart renascence. So an invalid rises
to try the ligatures, the veins which were like to have
rotted, and shuts his eye from the yellow light he had
almost lost.

In towns, walking the marble of gallery floors, sitting
with orchestras clad in black, we yield to the marshalled
force of art, of music and pictures. We forget that the
matter of art was first perceived by organs worn in or on
the body of every man. We are like squashes grown in

the corn, one side white and flat with lying against the earth. Certain of our senses are so stunted that, if they could be realized by sight, we should find them repulsive. We do not feel with the surface of our skin, for instance, or smell, with the hundredth part of our power. We hear only certain sounds, and they the loudest. We see only print and oncoming motors.

That accounts for my agitation now. My senses are so many inert grubs brought out from bark. The water rolls, and one side of the roll is green but the other flashes light. The wind blows, but not against the First National Bank. It strikes my naked back, sucking at my armpits as I lift the paddle, brushing my wrists and my navel as if with the breast-feathers of some creature very soft. The sun distils a smell from cedars: it heats their oil. Leaves, like flowers, have a smell, and bark is pungent as ginger. Fields have their odor and thickets theirs, thickets so dense that the seasons find no elbow-room and overlap. While June declares the shape of new leaves November is still soaking others, beating out of them a different smell in the same rain.

The man who has to get all of this at once has much to do. He is not the lad who just now stepped from his car. Five hundred yards downstream I understand already (and better than sailors themselves) why sailors jeer at clerks and cobblers; why they feel that their right to raise hell on shore is a divine right.

Noon comes with its seal of heat and the big heron is

29

slow on his wing. He scoops as if he were counting. Buzzards float high in a ball of specks that moves within itself but hangs in place, like snow about the castle I once had in a transparent globe. Doves blow in their hollow reeds. The roosters crow. Bull frogs mute their call but keep their posts. . . .

Even at midday the water is sweet. The air at its surface is cool to my hand as draft from a pane in winter. But the sun falls on the glistening wheat and on my head and I nod and I stare at the current. My eyes lose their power to fix themselves on objects close at hand. Flowing water and climbing flame bring this content. They lay down this hickory back-log of content that after dawn still has its eye of coal in the violet ash.

We pass a cave in the bluff, the air of its wide mouth full of phoebes as of bees about a hive. Over the convex face of the rock the wild rose blooms. And the whole scene lies doubled over the water, as you see yourself on the ball of a horse's eye. We come to a landing where a yellow road winds out of the wood from either side, its ribbon cut by the river. There is a solid ferryboat moored in the hem of foam, waiting for the horn, for those whose way for a quarter of a mile will have no dust. There is the keeper's house, with his yard of phlox and rose and tumbling puppies. Here are his children rushing to know the name of our town and its county; to ask where we got that boat and what does one of them fetch; to observe that they kain't no water git in hit nohow; to count out eggs from a split-cane basket; to splash water in our jug from pappy's

30

grave-voiced well. They watch us off from the ferry, between their legs the fat pups, crabwise, tongues a-lolling. One of them pokes his nose to the buzzing foam, starts back barking and as quickly stops, sitting to watch us with the rest.

This night we are kept from camping on the bank we choose. A lop-eared native steps from the brush as we land, to explain that he sure ain't wantin' to cause no hard feelin's, but that the folks on both sides of the river have agreed to keep off strangers; cattle and hogs have been missing. I point out that the number of either with which we might make off in a canoe . . . but he interrupts and begins what he had said before. We push off, crestfallen as one is to find a rustic shorn of his principal charm—his welcoming smile and open gate. Here on the lower Osage some of the inhabitants are peasant types, men whose passion it is to possess and not to share. Towards the headwaters the traveller begins to find the hill-type, the mountaineers of the Ozarks. For them all persimmons are free as the ripening frosts that whiten to either side of the property line. Rocks are free and the water that courses over them in storms is free. I ask a man: "Will you let me put my tent here?" And he answers: "Boy, this here 10,000 acres is all mine. Reckon that'll do ye a spell?" His mare shifts her footing as he moves in the saddle to look down at me. Wind stirs in the leaves as I grin up at him. Silence between us. But our hearts are as quick as a branch from which a squirrel has jumped. We have the same *patria*. We are com-patriots. We are willing to share, as if we were blood brothers.

Driven now from land set apart in the county book "Proceeding thence along a line north," we disembark downstream to camp in underbrush and mud. The moon comes long before dark, rising superb and unexpected at the tent door. It sends a path through the green reflections of the willows like a comet's tail, ending in the ball of the orb itself. Dusk fades. The willows fade, and the path remains on the water. Dark flickers run through it—leaves and sticks, driftwood, the little hollows of unequal current. Bull frogs like buck niggers try their membranous bass. The alders tilt their discs to the silver light.

We slide off the edge of the canoe to bathe, and know how far we are from towns as the cold water strikes our knees, invades our crotch, the cleft of our buttocks, the hollows of our armpits; as it draws about our necks the circle of fine thread beneath which the body seems dissolving like a pill.

I spread my toes warm and grateful in the sleeping bag. When slumber comes the moment is not marked, yet the arrival of a bullet could not be more prompt. Before the setting of the moon we are wakened by a sound which might appropriately have come from a thing as tall as the Trojan horse. It is the whip-poor-will on a branch at my head. It has been a long time since I slept with a little cat-whiskered whip-poor-will. I had forgot what she can do with a mouth and a cubic inch or so of lung. It

32

startles, it freshens, it uncovers an awareness, as in music
an unorthodox sequence; in painting, diversion from rep-
resentation. It is so fresh, indeed, that lying flat on my back
by the river I do not think of our art, but of that of the
Osage—his white swan "swinging up and down on the
waves of water"; his rattlesnake that "talks from bunched
grass with the sound of wind when it blows from cedar":
his cray-fish, "the cloven-handed": his "little mottled
lynx" and the puma that uproots *tsé-wa-the*, the chinquapin
bulb, "with a quick movement of his foot." How dismiss
as savages folk who speak so of the Great Elk (he-never-
absent-from-an-important-act): "the ball-like muscles of
his rumps they are the hills of earth; the bone of his back
the ridge of hills. The tines of his antlers are the streams,
the bases of his antlers the loose rock of earth. The curve
of his neck is the dip of hills." Why fail to acknowledge
the talent of men who describe the bear "near the time of
the great division of days," knowing he must sleep, seeking a cave, settling his haunches to rest "conscious of
having found for himself a room most pleasing and satis-
fying"; slumbering with "toes gathered together in folds,
with overhanging cheeks, until the birds sing and the land
is overspread with mist"? Surely David the Psalmist and
Solomon . . .

We come to another camp at noon. Why wait for night?
If you run and have running after you a bull that has
lowered the knives of his horns, you have decided wisely.
If between your backside and his brow is sufficient space,

33

you enjoy success. Elsewhere speed is confession of failure. Every object about you is valueless until you come. Each has for you only the price you can give it. Some men are frightened at this, seeing that worth is a dew which must fall from the red cloud of their own heart, and they back away from the whole problem. They "step on it." They say one village is fifty minutes away from another. They live in a hollow tube of wind. The Lord their God is a prodigal God and must be amazed to see them hostages in the land he gave them.

We in this boat, being now neither in storm and rain, nor at sunrise, nor at the setting of the moon, in any hurry whatever, are free to camp at noon and not at night. This is a good place. It has a high bank, with toes of trees for stairs. It lies in a long cleft of rock closed with an amphi-theatre of hills. It is flat, covered with grass that has grown fine and tall and fallen back. It would be a bad place for an ant to travel, seeing that he would wish to walk the brow of earth and not waste time along green arcs in air. On the other hand, there is room—soft room—for many a deer to make his bed. A row of elms stands by the river side, regular as on a gentleman's avenue. We pitch our tent beneath the high sweep of their boughs. It does not mar the scene. It is green.

Below, where the canoe is moored, my boys swim. Their white limbs seem bigger in the water, and at the water line where they emerge obliquely, natural size again. Black butterflies desert the mud to flutter at their shoulders. When the swimmers are cold they place their fingers on

the rim of the canoe and stiffen themselves, throwing over
one leg then the other. The canoe rocks. She takes their
bodies like a big and patient female. She takes anything.
They are her boys.

Between their outbursts of splashing and laughter there
is silence absolute, except for wind in leaves and the squeal
of boughs that rub. Being disposed to let go, to let con-
tentment well up within me, I seize upon that sound,
remembering the rope swings of childhood. I recover the
upward rush, the flexing of knees, the burn of the rope in
my fingers. The ground has little power over me. I can
distort it sickeningly. And I can fall back in a wild arc
not seeing my way, the wind parting my hair behind. It
is a better feeling now than then. Now it knows itself. It
knows what it is holding off with its other hand, with its
power like a tide running.

Now I must talk with a farmer who has come up. There
is always a farmer who has come up. But I am well content.
Pleasure had from a good host is pleasure double. And
if the host have the shoulders of a truck-driver, the eyes
of a child, with the tongue of a patriarch, no harm is done.
I answer his questions patiently, intending to have my
turn, meaning to draw at the pipe when in good time it is
handed me. I tell him the name of my family (my gens,
my tribe). I say how my county is called. I have no secret.
I do not hide the origin of my boat or fail to tell how
much one of them fetches. When he discovers that they
kain't no water git in hit nohow, I smile with him. Haste
is bad. The abrupt is the ill-bred.

35

But I am rewarded. He tells me that on this spot where I am camped was a steamboat landing once. This in the day when roads there were none. When the farm-wife, needing a bolt of ticking, got word to the captain somehow. And the boat blew its whistle and the boat left. Saint Louis gave up the cloth at the captain's word. And the boat returned and woke the woods with its whistle. The wife made a pillow with a yard of her ticking. It was warm to the head of her man in the starry length of night. . . .

Now, to take a blunt steamer from the Saint Louis levee; to make her butt her way to the wild Missouri, to the Osage; to avoid snags and sawyers and keep off bars; to read the surface of the water accurately when there was only one chance, even by moonlight, even when waves sent water streaming to the panes of the pilot house; to land, to cut cords of ash when your fingers would not close about the helve and the flesh of your face went tight with cold—all that was hard. "Manifest destiny" was a politician's phrase. It was grandiose and easy. Destiny made manifest by man took a different toll. We cross bridges not knowing what wheels lurched there to the ford. From roads we see the prairies and woods, unable to say who fell there coughing, with blood driving air from his lungs. My car in an hour exceeds their wagon's stint of days. I am grateful and ashamed. Something finer than I and my kind should have bloomed from so much effort.

And what monument stands on this grass? What lettered shaft? Only the grass itself. A farmer's word and a row of trees. The bark has grown over the bite of chains, the planks of the warehouse fallen. The moisture has eaten them utterly. The grass that grew under them white is green; it walks thickly over the site. Young heifers stand hoof-deep and let us scratch between their horns. There are no chariot ruts in the floor of an Osage Pompeii.

When the farmer is gone I walk to a tiny stream that flows to the river, yellow with gravel and very clear. At a point where it spreads to a pool about the size of a tub, I take off my clothes and use it for one. The two frogs and the young turtle that see me do not mind my nudity. I step to the bank to tarry in the wind to dry, grateful for this moment when by exception it is sweet to have flesh, to stand living in it, holding it to air that moves from woods.

Dusk pulls down about the tent. The elm boughs fold behind us hemming the river from night, olive, silver and rose. A time comes before dark when reflections of the opposite shore are more clear than the objects themselves; when over the mirror of water moves the shape of a heron we cannot see, level and slow among the stars. This bird, these stars on water, are seen more plain than in a ground lens. This moment floats out of chaos, a tight bubble that nothing holds back. So from the roof of caves a cold drop with its load of lime precise and infinitesimal. So from the surface crash of the sonata a great theme snuffed out at first, then as a fountain starts, springing upward full, whispering because it is very strong.

Black night comes, and the moon shouldering itself

from the hill. The long light slants beneath the elms showing the green of the grass, the useful monument of the
steamboat men. To amuse ourselves for a moment before
we take to bed, to avoid confessing that we want an excuse
to wander through this light, we hunt the small frogs
about the pool where I bathed. They are silent as we
approach. They resume their song as we stand. They are
sheepish in the beam of the flashlight. The one we catch
has a triangular waist and heart-shaped hips, like the
bodice of François Premier. It is rubbery and cold. It has
a porcelain glaze. It is rigid, knowing that its legs—its life
—are in a grasp. We return to our camp, to the fire standing up in separate locks of flame, tiny under the vast-
arched elms by their reach of river. We sleep, and make
in the grass a spot where an elk might have rounded
his bed.

Time is gone. Or Time is altered. There is no convict
lockstep of days which are single and parts of a chain. The
days are a flowing whole; the month a mist about us dense
at the heart, feathering toward its edge. The years surround us and move with us. They do not cut us off. This
day, whatever day it is or would have been in town, is
spent on the river wide now, like a lake. It is astonishing
to find what they can do together, the wind and the river.
There are whitecaps. There are hollows that open chop-
pily before our prow. To avoid the fatigue of keeping to
course by paddle we turn on our motor, the little hornet
that purrs beneath the stern. Now the boat is able to exe-

cute her will. The arc of her nosing side-to-side is reduced
by her speed in the forward line. She moves on not accepting nonsense. She pushes the waves in the face, the waves
that run back like puppies whose bark has failed to
frighten.

The wind is high and whistles in my ears, but the sun
is bright. There are fleets of "pop-corn" clouds, high
packed from the level dew-point. They diminish in per-
spectives obviously so vast that I sense the curvature of
the globe. With a fine pair of glasses I live in the swaying
figure-eight of the lenses—looking into the caverns of
cloud as from the window of an air-liner. I remember that
the Osages have a collection of poems to clouds which
they call: "Songs of the High Hills."

Toward afternoon, the wind being dead and the river
serious, we come to an island. For a reason I cannot trace
—or rather, for no reason, since it is purely a revelation—
I know that this island will be diamond-shaped, that this
is the back of an island of which I know the lower tip.

Years and years ago, when we first began to feel independent in automobiles and could go in them "right out
into the country," I was taken frequently along a road
which crossed the Osage near its mouth and, climbing a
hill, kept in sight of the river for a while. Here I could
look down at the water, well-defined as if it were solid
glass or silver in its bed, a vein of ore exposed. I could see
a dam, a lock, and a colony of government houses trim
on a lawn in the wild woods by the shore. Into these I was

39

sure I could thrust my hands as I played with my Noah's ark, as I moved the houses of my toy town and its trees, the triangular pines set in a disc of wood. But the town I already owned. I had no islands. On the glass of the river above the dam lay a cluster of islands, exactly hemmed, graceful as fruit among the leaves. The largest was diamond-shaped, set prow-and-stern with the current. As my bones grew longer and my voice grew queer, and my hair, though Mother gripped my chin and brushed it hard, would not lie down, I was again and again allowed to see the island—but never to go into it; to walk among its trees; to see the water flowing by to either side. It became a significant point of earth to me, as certain spots are marked by the Coastal Survey. It was a boundary corner, a *thule* reached by my soul which pivoted here proceeding south-southeast to a point then unrevealed. Had I been removed from earth, shut in a cañon of the High Hills, set to sing in a cleft of the thunderheads, I should have remembered the island. The light of memory would have converged upon it. It would have stood up, beaded in the fog.

Now, the island I see before me is indeed that island. Rounding its diamond tip there are landmarks in plenty by which to check. Truth compels me to admit, however, that it differs in no way from any of a dozen others. It has no lawn of Valhalla, no secular trunks to stand in the gloom of mist. There is in fact no mist. It is afternoon and the leaves are listless. Yet what I recall and not what I see is the truth. This plain land lying here, wet where the water has fallen since morning, is a mirage, a temptation of the Devil. The true isle is the isle that sat the stream like a salver, caught and like to move again, so full of motion was its motionlessness. . . . There is only one mistake. Before, when I passed on the heights, the island was inhabited by nymphs. They are not here now with their ivory limbs and their vapid smiles that seemed so lovely. I find instead the faces of folk who rode over the hill to see the island with me—my grandfather, his shoulders and beard, his well-chiselled temple and delicate hands: my mother who died with beauty still on her, who threaded a crowd with ease because the crowd made way. It is very strange. No one had told me that they lived in the island.

At the dam below, the river, being very high, is but little hindered in its speed. Over the top of the concrete line is a polished dip. Below it rapids are boiling hoarsely. We manœuvre to the gate of the lock to wait for the attendants. Four of them it seems are required to open the way for us. They are so lanky, so slow, they have so perfectly the accent of their soil that they stand out oddly against the official tidiness of the lock and its residences. Like all countrymen taken from fields to work for the "govmint" they are at once pompous and sheepish. As they push the wheel that locks the upstream gate, they stop and lean and forget us in their talk. . . . Lord, boy, y'ain't aimin' t'put out no fire? . . . As the lower gate opens, they remember that, as a matter of record, they must have my name and that of my boat. The first they understand, though it is not a name of this county. But when I stand yelling mischievously (over the roar of the rapids, over the carillon of echoes rolling in the lock): *"Ni-sho-dse! Ni-sho-dse!"* the lock-master leans out with open mouth, head tilted to one side, eyes closed, his pencil poised. As we are drawn out by the current I see his lips form: "God damn it . . ." and words which probably are: "that ain't no name!"

We pass the mouth of the Maries, a gentle stream whose beauty is no less because its name is garbled. Like the upper Osage, it was called by the French *le Marais des Cygnes,* and for brevity's sake *Marais*—which luckless word was written by the English *Marias, Marys* and finally *Maries.*

Last night the moon was abruptly dimmed and there was storm. A pillaging wind, an angry river and the moored boat rearing like a horse in smell of bear or fire. The cottonwood leaves made a waterfall. The long flag of thunder was unfurled. And through it all we lay on our backs in the mobile and resonant tent alone with earth, fire, air and water. This is hard until one has the habit. Tension brings into play nerves dormant normally, wakens whole sectors of ourselves that comforts lull at home. How to become, without notice, one with the crouched cat, the hen-turkey under a snow-bent limb, the buck deer lowering his tines from the mingling sleet? How did the *coureurs-de-bois* do, and the fur hunters? The men with

a little salt in a bag and a little meal in a bag, bound for
the Rockies? The men with one pack-horse, walking to
Texas? Did they, naked of a rainy night, turn backs to
wind like deer or cattle? We have at least the tent, almost
transparent in the bottle-green flares. It turns the rain,
or most of it. In it we may sleep again, lapped by the river,
our cheeks nudging the breasts of silence when the wind
is dead. By its door in the thin-washed air under the uncertain sun we may, this morning, perform the miracle of
coffee.

The Osage near its mouth is wide and exuberantly
wooded. Fixed hills flow at you from all sides but one—
in front is a long blue line which would puzzle us greatly
if we did not know it to be the north shore of the Missouri.
In that interval of haze lies the great stream, and not in
name only. It is there actually, with tons of eager water
shouldering, butting its way down from the country of
Crow and Mandan, yellow and fat with the soil of plains.
It waits like a relay runner ready to take the baton from
the Osage, running with little backward-looking steps
until we come.

For us this drama is made more quick by sudden dark
and storm. Sensing already the hidden Missouri, we are
called upon to sit in wind sensing also storm. The first
drops come singly, so that the bias of their path is clear;
then bodily the shower falls, making the river boil. The
one of my companions who is French and wiry and dark
sits in the stern lifting his face to the rain, grinning at the

43

flares, shrugging at the green swells that lift us and drop us, singing at the top of his voice, *Salut demeure chaste et pure*. He is behaving as his ancestors did in these waters, and his song in this clean rain at the meeting of rivers is less out of place than at first it might appear.

The storm, having scoured us well, goes on. We see it far off, a pearl dust over the Missouri. We pass on the left a hamlet called Osage City. "Here, to use the language of the country," says Major Long in 1819, "a town has been *located*, and the lots disposed of in Saint Louis; $50 to $180 each." Those were days when the young Republic was biting out of the West chunks larger far than she could chew; blessed days when there was a frontier, a cupboard whence the government drew peppermints for malcontents, a clean rough place where any boy could "succeed" if he "grew up with the country." No capital investment, no taxes, no overproduction—nothing but his woman and his rifle and his independence which, for unalloyed impudence, remains unequalled in the world. In those days the West was visited by a race of men called since sharpers, promoters, confidence men, who by fair means or foul— but probably fair (it was so easy!)—acquired a tract of land. Sometimes there was an honest trading post on it, with a coon's tail to its cap, and Indians who, when their hands were dirty, wiped them on their hair. Sometimes there was only a swamp that smelled of a vase in which stems have rotted; a green mushiness known to the white wild swan. Returning East, the new proprietors announced the birth of towns, "queen cities" of the untapped interior.

Description of these drew heavily upon the language of the Old Testament and the New, and the Protestant hymnal. As proofs beyond dispute, maps were unfurled, and wood-block prints of palace yards having fountains.

If Osage City was one of these, the investment of the Saint Louisans has long ago been written off a loss. The "city" is a pleasant hamlet that opens an eye in its dozing to watch you by.

Beyond it, on the right, white against the green hills, stands a larger village, Bonnot's Mill. We make our way toward it, toward a rain-washed scene lying now in a burst of light; whatever it has of commonplace reduced by the cool, by the mirroring drops that stand like dew. We land, nosing into a collection of craft, some rotted and half-sunk, some sturdy and home-made, worthy, but with the country look of a man who has had his hair cut in a cross-roads shop.

If the village were much less sweet than it is, we should be excited still by this landing, by this entrance into the particular, the fixed, the wind-sheltered—we arriving from the green expanse, the full horizon and the cardinal points, from space where the wind walks up and down in the earth like the Devil in the Prayerbook.

Before we have moored we are met and escorted by a flotilla of new-hatched ducks that move on the water with the ease of drops of oil. They are ridiculous balls of fuzz. But they have nonetheless a miraculously bright eye in the slender blade of their heads; a jet that has the light of babies' eyes, of puppies' eyes, of monkeys' eyes. After our days in the bowl of horizons it seems most happily concentrated.

After the ducks it is a garden—such is the shoreline that we had to land in a garden—with hollyhocks, primroses and a tangle of poppies. Then a gate to the village street, one of the streets of the lower town wedged in the cleft of hills like an old gunstock in the fork of limbs. This settlement was in its origin French, one of a chain that stretched west of Saint Louis on the Missouri. This one, like the others, was invaded by Germans during the 1840's. It grew a little, and with steamboat and railroad became an important depot for freight, carried thence about the country in wagons. However, it did not grow too much. As wind passed over it, twisting trees on the crests above it, the wind of business went by too. The Germans, if they altered the foreignness of the French, brought their own, so that Bonnot's Mill is trim and neat by its rivers. Its street smells of its lumber yard; its galleried store buildings and the *Hotel Dauphine* look like a collector's "early print." The houses are too smothered in bloom to please or to trouble with their architecture.

There is a lane we climb, leaning forward, for the lane is steep. At its end the church stands high. Before the door, under a pitched roof like the roof of a well house a Christ hangs on a cross. He is chalk-white above the blood roses that rise to his knee. Inside, two porcelain angels, pink and white and gold, offer the holy water in porcelain shells. Wasps are making the stations of the cross, butting their heads and buzzing. A Madonna of Prague stands in a glass case, her green dress stiff, with lace falling back from her upraised hand. A crown is perched over her baby face. All about stand saints that seem to have stopped their converse at our step. Their smiles are rapt. Here is the still and wind-sheltered again, and the bright concentration as in the little duck's eye. Without duplicating it precisely, we can share the emotion of men of the Iceland fleet who come home to France, out of the winds that blow from the Pole; out of the northern sunrise, sulphur and pearl; home to the rock of Brittany; home to the chapel where there is no wind, where candle flames have the shape of hearts and are quite still.

The lane ends at the church, but the hill goes on to a crest from which we have again the full horizon. To our left the Missouri rolls in a bend, eager out of the west, and its great bulk is so bright in the sun that it offers no detail. Opposite where it flows before us, a single bluff rises from the plain, oddly isolated. Perhaps in ancient days the path of the river lay around it, not, as now, before it. But to the French settlers no such explanation occurred. They called it the *Côte-sans-dessein*, by which, in their colonial tongue, they meant to imply that the *côte* (the hill) was strange, peculiar, without reason. There on that site was a trading post, fort and village, called also *Côte-sans-dessein*. There in 1808 came a certain Jean Baptiste Roi from Bout-de-l'isle in Canada. There (probably at the instigation of Auguste Chouteau) he set up a post

47

where he could receive pelts from countries drained by the Missouri and the Osage. Nothing remains of his village, destroyed by floods and by battles. But it was once an "ultimate outpost" of white civilization, the remotest settlement west of Saint Louis. It was important enough at the time of the War of 1812 to merit attack by the Sacs and Foxes, allies of the British. The engagement has remained famous in local history for the part which French women took in the defense, especially the wife of the commandant. When the roof of the fort was in flame and when no water, milk or wine was left, she had an immortal idea. She "produced from the urinals a fluid" which extinguished the blaze—and the following year was presented by certain young blades of Saint Louis with a silver replica of the original vessels, suitably inscribed.

Below us, parallel with the Missouri for a while, is the Osage—and to the right its mouth, its joining with the Missouri. Within the hour we shall be there. We shall not know it on a map or make it out from a distant hill. We shall straddle it ourselves and give it fight. Under bluffs that stand like icebergs in the sun we shall move out to *Ni-sho-dse*, the Murky Water, Indian colored and a mile wide. At a given moment, still riding the waters of the Osage, we shall lose the old impetus, hesitate; then, as if freed of a weight, move on with the new. And in the pit of our bellies will be the feeling that must have prompted Marquette to write: "Thus we left the waters flowing to Quebec . . . to float on those that would henceforth take us through strange lands."

III

THE MISSOURI

# III

## The Missouri

THE MISSOURI RIVER is two thousand five hundred and forty-six miles long. The true banks in places are seventeen miles apart. It carries three times the sediment of the Nile. Now that Boulder Dam causes the waters which it restrains to clarify themselves in a lake, the Colorado is no longer the muddiest river in the world. That title falls to the Missouri. Its flow is brown with the soil of Montana, Dakota, Nebraska. You cannot wash your shirt in it, or your hair. By all the tribes that knew it the Missouri was given a name meaning muddy or murky water. The Illinois in their Algonquian language called it *Pekitanoui*—as Marquette records. But the Illinois also attempted to render the name the Missouri Indians had given the river in their Siouian tongue, the name which they also took for their tribe: *Ni-shu-dsi*. Of this, adding their typical Algonquian prefix *ou*, the Illinois made *Oumissourit*. It was *Oumissourit* that Joutel picked up among the Illinois, setting it down in 1687. It is of *Oumissourit* that the French and Spanish and English in turn have made *Missouri*.

Yet the Missouri is not nasty. It is simply fecund. Physical creation, as any midwife can tell you, involves an unsightly mess. The result is always troubling in its implications. It is always curious, sometimes beautiful. It humbles all but the callow, the selfish.

When, in the right season and in the good place, the Missouri can slacken a little in its speed, it brings forth. It drops sediment that may become an island. Perhaps it is in midstream where rarely, of course, it can remain visible except at low water. Perhaps it is below the lip of a tributary, or along a shore of the off-current side. There it gathers slowly about the fertilized core, though for long it is nearly "without form and void." At high water it is flooded. Chunks of its edge give way and dissolve. Floods recede, leaving a new layer of mud that is first slimy, then rubbery. It is blue-green and chocolate colored. It cracks and curls, like the shingles of an old roof. But it "brings forth abundantly the moving creature that hath life." It is visited in numbers by the "fowl that may fly above the earth in the firmament of heaven"—the killdeer, the buzzard, the heron that walks precisely in the green gum. There is everywhere a turning and squirming on the belly; a trying of knees and wings; a revolving of eyes; a making of tracks and gluey trails; a crawling and hopping and flitting; an insemination and a laying of eggs. In pools left by retreating water fish lie bloated, stinking, but yielding to the whole the oil of their liver, the calcium of their bone.

There is in this teeming no hint of the cooling of the

sun, of the possible collision of earth with an astral body. There is no threat of the decline of the West, of the enfeebling of religion, of menace to the democracies. There is not even any suggestion that creation once created might be ranged and defined and made reasonable to man. Man comes, and as he walks the weight on his feet increases. There is a scurrying from him with squeaking, with hissing, with rattle of carapace. He leaves, and the male crawls to the female, placing in her body the sperm, or touching it to the eggs she has left in the sand.

Successive deposits of silt build the island high, so that finally, except for periods of very high water, it becomes land like any other. Buffalo and elk there are none to make their home here, to sink to the hock in sand as they climb from the ford. But wolves are left, and a few eagles. Inland on the highest ground appear thickets of willows, then of cottonwoods and sycamores. These in time make a topsoil, set in motion the forest cycle—the cycle which is interrupted by a farmer with axe and seed bag. This ground is now his. He calls it "made land."

Between the woods and the waterline rains carry down the mud, leaving on the surface sand that in the dry season is hot, gold, and crusty. On windy days it is carried off in a straight line, low over the water, to a point where it is diffused, spread upward in a yellow cloud. Such days are blue, blinding with light. The heat, the space, the wind combat and diminish thought.

The history of the Missouri is as long as its course. Yet we know little of the Indians for whom it was named.

They were of Siouan stock and shared in the second great migration of their kind. In this movement some halted on the shores of Lake Michigan (the Winnebagos), some on the upper Mississippi (the Iowas), and some (the Otos) continued to Nebraska. The Missouris themselves, by their tradition, settled first at the mouth of the river that bears their name, in a town which they later abandoned for another at the mouth of the Grand. It was in this second location that they were probably known to the first whites. They never prospered. Decimated by smallpox, conquered and dispersed (1798) by the Sacs and Foxes, some of the survivors cast their lot with the Kansas and Osages; others with the Otos, on whose reservation in Oklahoma the last full-blooded Missouri died long ago.

The river made its entrance into the lives of Europeans on a spring morning of 1673. Marquette, still shaken by his discovery of the Mississippi, reports that, floating on fine water, quiet and clear, he heard the noise of a "rapid." The sound was made at the junction of the Mississippi and a stream which he called, in the language of the Illinois, *Pekitanoui*. Wreckage of whole trees was ground up about the mouth, and "floating islands" came out at him with such speed that he hesitated to risk his canoe among them.

Following the discoverers came the young men of Canada. Aubert de la Chesnaye writes in 1697 that the Hurons are no longer needed as intermediaries in trade with tribes to the south. Four or five hundred Canadians, flower of the population, have taken over that function themselves. The letters of D'Iberville speak of these fellows in the Missouri country in the years 1703–1706. In 1795, when Trudeau headed an expedition from Saint Louis for the *Compagnie pour l'Exploitation du Haut Missouri,* single trappers and bush-rangers already knew the river well into Dakota. Such men were in the employ of Lewis and Clark when they fought their way to the Columbia, accomplishing almost furtively one of the greatest single feats of history. In the days which followed this official opening of the West, the Missouri was the first highway, linking the villages of the robe-collecting Indians of the northern range, the forts of the fur companies, with Saint Louis. Its procession of bull boats, flat boats, and finally the wood-burning steamer; its ice floes, floods, its bear and antelope, its swollen bodies of drowned buffalo floating, all have made a pageant not equalled again until the prairie schooners, the immigrant trains to Santa Fe, and, later, the cattle drives from Texas. The Missouri became, as has been said of the Oregon Trail, an American idea as well as a road.

The story of the river is stirring. This country of the West and South deposits topsoil and compost in mad plenty. It offers ample accommodation for hair roots and the central tap. Men who leave it, seeking "culture"— another, that is, than this—are thin-blooded creatures, the transparent lice that drop from the healthy stem. It is, after all, a convenience to have them congregated in great eastern centers.

## Where the Rivers Meet

If these are not frankly afterthoughts they are present today only in the background of our minds. Flushed from the green corridor of the Osage, we have suddenly much to do, little to say, and that little in the present tense. History, if we could speak of it, if the wind did not scoop words from our open mouths, if we were not listening for the lasso-crack of whirlpools, would seem less than motes in a shaft of light. We are kept, not by wisdom of our own, but by force of the water, from seeing history as a thing stopped. We take up visibly where the predecessor left off. For others the tidy conclusion, the tempered opinion. Our share is the muscle and bulge of the thing itself, the wind, the strong brown flowing.

We give ourselves wholly, at first, to the problem of navigation. No memory of peaceful stream, of lake or seacoast, serves one here except as a base from which to depart, meeting new conditions. We are in a vise from which there is no quick removal. To reach either shore, landing at a given point, would take time and a special skill. With the river at this stage our pilot knows that few swimmers in the world, thrown from the boat, could get to the dim bank. For this type of boating (how rococo the term seems now!) a man might prepare himself by riding the back of a stampeding buffalo. Let him straddle the humped back that was not meant to sit on. Let him look about when he can at the eyeballs, the red mouths, the miles of hard heads bobbing. Let him fill his ears with the unnatural thunder.

The Missouri for all its size is swift. Like a bear or an

alligator, it moves surprisingly. From shore it would seem to move uniformly along the whole breadth—a seeming which the novice had better get out of his head at once. Actually there is not a current, but currents, which twine and untwine; there are undertows; there is backwash that moves upstream as rapidly as the rest descends. There are dead spots where a part of the surface hangs back and the rest sweeps on; here it is well to have the long boat wholly within one or the other. There are places where various currents converge, shooting you forward—rarely where you want to go. There are, everywhere and constantly, whirlpools; small ones that open with the gurgle of an overturned jug; others, fifty to a hundred feet across, that blossom out with a loud kiss, boiling high in the center, descending in a funnel of bubbling rings that can pull down a log. Avoid these if you can. If you must cross them, or if they open under you, it is well to have strong men at the paddles. At best you will be driven tiresomely off your course; at worst you will be spilled in the foam with a canoe cushion which would probably hold you afloat for half an hour.

There is, besides navigation, another adjustment you must make in your first hour of the Missouri. Looking up from the water immediately surrounding, there pours over the edge of your mind the realization that you are no longer in reach of *objects*. The shores move apart and in their moving leave to either hand one half a mile of water, brown and unobtrusively striving—an adversary that has seen its chance and taken it, before alarm could

be given. There is no grip or toe hold. You are summoned
to abandon all your ways, to vacate yourself as in times of
inundations, of high wind, of bombardments and earth-
quakes. Your mind, accustomed to dimension and number, is reluctant to leave the warm feathers where it has
hollowed a place. It turns sickly back to the familiar—
here, the interior of the canoe—which is oddly precise, as
one finds one's piano in a field after the cyclone. This same
sensation you have had in Montana, driving at dusk and
by moonlight over the plains. There the earth in the midst
of a rolling, of a great swell, paused. It is scoured bare.
In the four directions and all their variants there is no
object to relieve the horizon or give it scale. You turn
then to the dashlight of your car, the bright point from
which must spread fanwise, lines to fill the universe. So
now I turn to the prow of the *Ni-sho-dse*, dropping my
eyes before the space beyond it, the hot light and piled
cloud which would knock out the walls of my skull to
make me domestic in new dimensions.

The storm which passed us so briskly this morning in
the Osage we have seen again at varying distances from us
during the day. Now it threatens to return. The wind
freshens and grows quick. Cottonwood leaves turn over
the fish-belly silver of their underside. Single blobs of
rain strike our heads, cold and splattering heavily, like the
droppings of birds. We pass the mouth of Loose Creek
(in French *Rivière à l'Ours!*) and, between the villages
of Saint Aubert's and Mokane, turn in for an island. We

hurl equipment from the boat and set up the tent, calculating every movement, like artillerymen with a field piece.

Then, after all, it does not rain. Driving a tide up the inlets, carrying off horizontally loose leaves and sand, the wind passes, leaving a beach pock-marked by drops. The big afternoon smiles. I place a blanket in the shade of the tent (anchored to the trunks of young cottonwoods) and, through the glasses, lie "living" in the clouds. They are huge and rise spreading from their own bulk, like a "slow-motion" of popping corn, making new abysses incredibly deep, fresh caverns of carved salt and wool. The area of the island, when I look back, seems too small to be safe.

Evening brings a scene which we should like to share with outlanders, particularly dwellers by a stream called the Hudson, who hear that the Missouri is muddy and think it is coffee-colored. If they could see it tonight, judging it not by a cup or a bucketful but by these cranberry-colored sunset miles; and now that dark has almost come, by the rose and olive, boiling silver! If they could see this brutal distance tinted acre by acre, dimmed by a mist that rises as from a spring!

Yet mud there is, in the water and out. We walk from camp, naked along the shore, to bathe. The sand under the balls of our feet has a curiously pleasant resistance. "Blisters" of water rise in our tracks; with a finger we can puncture them and make them run. Arrived at the end of the island where, like the tip of an upturned spoon, it dips to the water, we wade in—and to the ankle, to the knee, sink in a chocolate gumbo. We flounder and fall and slap at mosquitoes, laughing and cursing, pushing one another down to make sure that discomfort is general. Naturally there is no bath. We stand moistening our bodies gingerly, removing the day's sweat perhaps, but leaving in its stead a brown film. It is for this that one reads in the journals of the explorers: "Halted at the Gasconade to wash." "Ascended the Osage that the men might bathe."

We are refreshed by the contact of water nevertheless, and by the cold dusk. The disappointment of our swim is cancelled as we walk back, the wind on our wet thighs and shoulders. We are spry, less sleepy than we thought: fatigue was peeled back with the dirty shirt. We are seized with the silly delight of new lambs and April-born calves. We leap about. The better to emphasize our nakedness we adjust ties, hitch imaginary trousers, dispose of formal "tails" as we sit down. Each of my friends at the tent door bows, holding a flap that I may enter—each careful, however, to give me a vigorous boot as I reach the good angle, each hurling himself in after me, so that for a moment (strangled with mirth) I lie under a heap of cool struggling flesh. God himself must weep tonight seeing presidents of banks and prime ministers, and they mirrored in a table-top.

But the interior of the tent will not do. Its still jellied air after the movement without, its egg-shell ceiling after the roof of opening stars—no. Not even with threat of mosquitoes. We shall do what we try every night (well

60

knowing it will not work). Each spreads his sleeping bag
out on the sand, pulling its zipper up to the neck. Each
wears cotton gloves, and over his face (covering the opening of the parka hood) fits a piece of netting. So encum-
bered we might more simply get into a diver's suit. But
we are under the wide-open night. The night that is velvet
as a horse's nose. And out on the flat blade of the island
we have the sensation of being not under the stars, but
among them. I see them straight above and out of the
corner of each eye.

The adoration that floods me is religious. But this creed
is as wide as the dark. It fits loosely. I give myself to it
readily, spreading my toes, knowing I am rich and safe.
The petulant iconoclast is as puny here as the dogmatist.
Of the church who ever rejected what pertains to wheat
and fish and stars? The night is that it is.

Out of my first sleep I wake to find my lips fat as a
Senegambian's. Only one eye will open. My cheeks are
dotted with lumps. The lobe of one ear is enormous. The
netting has slipped from my hood. Mosquitoes have been
at me. They can scarcely leave me. Red-bellied and laden
they lie grunting, praising Allah for this lamb and rice.
My companions lie apart, still as a pair of dead troupers
to be shipped beneath the flag. Stars are high and few.
The river is furtive under the moon. I stumble to the tent,
hugging my bedding to keep its warmth.

We rise, with no resentment, at five in the morning.
Life is not resumed here with bared teeth as one puts on

61

wet clothes. Division of time is simple for us as for animals it is simple. There is a space of light and one of dark
and it is easy to see that both are good. They coincide with
our need to sleep, with our will to be up. It is heartening
and restful thus to fall in with facts of the cosmos. Something precious is diminished when, in towns, thick of
tongue and gummy-lidded, man keeps afoot at night;
when in the noxious close of bed he lies blind, renouncing
this boon of dawn. He loses an exhilaration still miraculously in reach—the rapture of those mornings when, a
child, he stepped to his mother's garden, feeling on his
shin-bone the small leaves, pulling to his face solemnly
the rigid lilies. Mornings when the edged air entered
under his starched shirt, the legs of his pants, playing over
the nipples of his skinny breast, shrinking his absurd little
sex-parts (sweet, to his mother, as the rest of him then).
Mornings when he walked back to his milk in the kitchen,
grave-eyed, with pollen on his nose.

Here we sit about the breakfast fire. With the smoke of
driftwood, the fishy mist of the river, our coffee has made
a good smell. How exaggerate these small good things of
earth. How are they small? On whose authority? Why
rush to important things? Who says they are important?
What do you remember of any twenty years? The chill
rubber of nasturtium leaves about your toes; the feel of
your hand in the small of a back; the odor of coffee about
a fire.

We seem to sit in a pocket of orchid mist, yet when we
move the pocket goes along. The willows disengage them-

selves and stand up wet, their boughs "working" with the live weight of red-wing blackbirds that climb to the tips, craning into the light. The air is chill and resonant and moves as from the bloom of fruit. Lying level on the sand I can see far over the water the streak of the water's running; the mist is packed close but it does not meet. As the sun climbs, as the wind is more aggressive, it is rifted. I have glimpses of the mainland to the right, picked out by a shaft that lurches in one beam from sun to earth: two round hills that overlap—from the shoulder of the largest, a white church tower. It fades at once but, for an instant, oversimplified and unnaturally intense, it sat in the wide end of its funnel of light.

We push off, past the mouth of the *Rivière aux Vases*— what a privilege, this morning's departure every morning! Once clear of the island we shrink to a dot so minute that surely an observer above would exclaim to see it divided four times, to find that it holds in its globe three men and a boat. We skirt islands. We round peninsulas whose bluffs are wooded on the face, whose round top or sides have fields of hay and pasture-wheat, suave as mole fur. They look clipped, rolled, "mannered" like a lawn. Yet to make a bright bulk at such distance the hay must be tall and thick and gray with dew. You would part it with both hands to walk through it; you would be wet to the hips.

The left bank (from midstream) is a broken line of dots, distinguishable at intervals, its flatness accentuated by rows of cottonwoods whose toothpick trunks (as in a Japanese print) do not seem to reach anything.

Past bend after bend we follow, entering vistas whose planes of distance, seemingly two-dimensional, stand out from one another flatly. The river moves in a long swell which carries us up, checking us, prow in air, and eases us forward. Where it is still it reflects like a well-mouth.

We shall be reproached, certainly, for failing to report that the Missouri is nasty, that everything a population does not want is dumped into it, that it is ugly and brutal. These facts concern not us but Committees on Flood Control and Pollution of Inland Waters. A Neapolitan, wandering from home, might well ease himself on the slopes of Vesuvius (where and with what glad abandon does the Neapolitan not ease himself?). But, viewing the little cone of his waste, your wonder would be only that a man could so relax on the brim of a crater. The force of the volcano would stand out disengaged the more freely for the pin point of your observation. So the Missouri. It is huge and strong. It turns under and converts to its advantage all that is thrown to it. It is less a river than a live force. And having great size, it has many moods, many aspects. This morning it flows with the color of apricots, moving over silver. It turns from us thickly in round lips, with the roll and pause of a substance heavier than water.

Its silence about me is rich and crumbly. Yet it is active. It draws and polarizes. The quiet and the beauty are sad with foretaste of the nostalgia I shall feel when I am no longer where there is a moving field of water. The back caves, the upper and outer pockets of my being are filling with recollection without line or profile, like a music coherent in the mind, never yet on the tongue. Under the weight of roofs in the midst of talk it will thaw, flow and fill me with a running and lapping. Talk will irritate. It will seem to be taking place between trains. A gabble which presently will not need to be remembered.

Requiring supplies, we attempt to put in at Chamois. There exists a village landing, but here, as always, it is invisible to those who do not know it. The little river towns squat like quail in furrows. They are nameless except on maps. They have no ten-foot sign, no electric eye that opens and closes to show you where they are. Their idea of location, identification, of transportation to and from, is tempered by the gait of seasons, the roomy anonymity of fields. Approaching such a place by motor you clip around a bend and down a hill (out of habit) as fast as you can. Your heart stops as you see, halted squarely in the middle of the road ahead, a model-T. You jam the brake, and, as you creep past in the room that is left, you see the driver leaning from the wheel. He is talking to a man on the gallery of a house—a man who has been called from the table, because he is wiping his mouth with the flat of his hand. He yells (as from one horizon to another): "We air a-goin to git into that upper fo'ty tomorrow. You boys want to be at the house come sun-up.

Heah?" Then, before you have quite rounded the car in the road, it starts up, nearly taking you broadside. The driver is not a man on a numbered highway proceeding in given time from point to point by map. He is an inhabitant of the broad earth.

Missing the Chamois landing we nose up between mainland and island in a channel so like a bayou with its reedy teeming, its banks no longer water and not yet soil, that we give up the idea of mooring ashore and tie up to a line of piles. Below the high bank we can see nothing. But I know that a settlement is close, as I know from an open drawer that a mouse has been there. The man-smell of villages is made up of the twang of wood fires, kerosene, and a third component hard to place but close to the odor of milk. In Missouri or Arkansas, Tennessee or Kentucky, it does not vary. Possibly it is the American settlement-smell, conjuring images of the rambler on its trellis, the outhouse under the grapes, bread, and thoughtful smoke.

Alfalfa at the top of the bank is shoulder high, heavy with blossom and bees. Once clear of it we find ourselves in a road edging fields. As always, coming in from the river, we are astounded by the tranquillity of the village —its chimney, its loaf, its larkspur and rose, its house cat on the ledge. An old lady tending her plants looks up. An old man smoking his pipe looks up. Both say: "Howdy." That is cordial. Brief, but enough until the stranger makes the next move.

In the stores tradesmen itch to know all about us.

"You boys a-fishin'?"

66

# The Missouri

"You boys off a boat?"

They look at us as at stratosphere fliers, though the river is at their door. We have the day before us, but they hurry as they fill out our list. They are as excited as if they were going with us. They are friendly, almost affectionate. Their hearts are plump with sound meat and oil, as kernels in the year of a good crop. We take leave of them in an air of joviality, of relaxation from the usual, of indulgence and complicity.

Trudging back in the road along the bayou we are halted by a man who inhabits, evidently, a houseboat moored at the bank. He is small, gray in hair and stubble, with three dark fangs for teeth. But his eye is blue and deep in its socket. The beak of his nose has a good line. His little boy peers from behind a heap of nets. The woman has fled at our approach, but she is listening. One of her red arms is at a curtain of the boat.

The hands of city women, from lack of use and from smearing with ointments, frequently look less like hands than the paws or flippers of something floating in a jar. Not so the hands of country women. They have pulled at the udders of cows and gathered eggs still hot from the flesh of the hen. They have held up, joined, the feet of a baby, while they powdered his little chafed rump with cornstarch. They pare whole apples without breaking the peel; so squirrels turn nuts with their forefeet. From habit of the task they pick at things constantly, smoothing cloth that is already smooth. If they must be still they lie open in the lap, offering yet to help.

# Where the Rivers Meet

The man is amused that we have "packed" water jugs out from town. He says he will be dogged. And he turns to spit where he will not hit us. He has always drunk from the river—motioning to the bayou lolling, bubbling, sucking with its nigger lips at the mud. He is by trade a fisherman. This morning he found his hoop net (set in the gut of a channel) so packed with fish that he "could not have got another in behind." He "rolled it out like a barrel." It is plain that I shall have to manœuvre this interview deftly to its end, without purchase of a chunk of carp that none of us would touch.

This man, this woman and child have never lived on shore except like this. Always in the houseboat. They know the canebreaks of the delta, the pelicans and the palms. They have seen the cypress knees of the Red River and the Arkansas. The Cumberland and the Des Moines are so many rooms in their house. For them a great section of the globe is home. The boat is a kind of chiffonier in which they keep their things. Pittsburgh and Saint Paul, Cairo and Calico Rock, Natchez, the Bayou Saint Jean— their least word sets off this carillon of names.

I examine the little boy with uncritical envy. At his age, to be sure, I might have whimpered, given to drink the tepid mud of the bayou, made to eat only fish and meal (with hog and green corn, stolen from farmers). But he is as agile as a water spider in his rowboat. He knows, as a tree knows it, the river stung and howling with storm or broad beneath the moon. In summer he sees where nets are sunk; he helps to pull them up, and watches

through their mesh the tail and eye, the open mouth of
fish. In winter he plays in the sand roads that skirt the
bank, green with equisetum, red with cardinals, white
with the flag of cottontails. He knows the plain of the ice
floe, the tilting, dipping, grinding of the cakes with the
sound of coarse salt running. Stooping down and looking
over, he sees the great blocks waiting in a currentless bay,
like the heads of many sheep before a gate. Except for the
old ones who mated, and begot him in the boat, men are
rare in his life. He behaves before them as before other
large mammals. He runs to make his examination from the
shelter of the brush, fluent as a fox among the branches.
Trapped, he would chew off his foot. He will never be
captured. The umbilical cord was his last tether.

Clear of the willows of the bayou at noon, into the hot
width of the Missouri once more, we consult the government signs, placed on the shore or at the end of jetties
(giving distance to a fraction of a mile from the mouth of
the river). We resented these at first as intrusions upon
our solitude. Such touchiness is felt only by the newcomer,
appraising in terms of his garden the privacy of the open.
He would not want a sign in his petunias. But in such a
theatre as the valley of the Missouri, whose roof and
walls are merely sensed, divined as the end of the sky
is known at night, the little sign does not insist upon its
presence. We give it no more heed than the buzzard
feather fallen in willows, or, after dark, the moving light
of transport planes among the stars. It is even a welcome

point of reference. By its small size and great exactitude it increases our apprehension of space, as when we drop a line to camp from Vega or Aldebaron.

Here the sign reads 105.3. Looking on ahead I know that yonder, about even with a certain bluff on the right, there will be another, 103.5. It will mark the mouth of the Gasconade River. Of this I am sure from a book in my lap, sole volume of my baggage:

LIGHT LIST
Lights, Buoys and Daymarks
MISSISSIPPI AND OHIO RIVERS
And Their Tributaries
Fifteenth Lighthouse District
Washington, 1938.

Whether or not it was their intent, the men who compiled this list of names and distances have made a history of the river valleys; not pedestrianly, factually, but after the manner of poets, with piquant indirection, in language that like a fern bed, or a bank of mint, turns up odors immediately for the nose: Tavern Rock, Caney Creek, Buck Island Foot Buoy: Cypress Bend Upper Light, Blood River Lower Light: Hog Point, Cowgap, Yellow Dog Landing: Broom Corn, Backbone, and Mudle Hurdle Log Yard: Piasa Bluff, Cap au Grès, Hanging Dog, Tea Table: Dear Plain, Coon Creek and Leatherwood Shoals: Big Barn, Rat Sack, Sans Souci Bar Light: Tobacco Patch, Chalk Bluff, Cinq Hommes Cut-off: Boatwright Chut,

# The Missouri

Bonhomme Island: Old Maid's Bar Buoy and Duck River Suck Buoy: Standing Rock, Cul-de-Sac, and Dundee Towhead: Crazy Point, Lady Gay, and Millrace Slough Buoy.

Such names are our surest liaison with the past. They continue in vigor when common nouns drop, preserving much that we should not lose. Here at this joining of midland rivers they have the odd bite of the frontier—the marjoram and blood, the thyme and leather—when Saint Louis cheered the lurching wagon trains; when Arkansas was a deer-trodden ridge, Illinois a sea-roll of high grass; when in Kentucky there was a first mingling of courtliness with rifle-toting. Animals, forests, then men (the tobacco patch, the corn clearing). Later the brick house, the ferry and millrace, the wood yard, the planter's landing; a poising of Americans before the last West—the plains, the bare knobs, the high passes, the thin line where the water meets the sky.

No matter how else the baggage is packed, this list of lights will be on top. On bright mornings it will lie in my lap, its page to wind. On days of storm it will fall to the floor when I throw up my arm, seeing too late that I am to have in my face the grainy force of a wave. In calm it will hear the happy call:

"Portage des Sioux ahead, left, one mile!"
In driving rain with the floor a-slush; with our necks wet, our behinds wet, our feet wet; with visibility nil in the dust of spray, it will hear the pilot ask:

"What mile was that?"
And out of the prow, dully, from under a poncho:

71

# Where the Rivers Meet

"Petticoat Riffle Upper Daymark."

"Crossing to land! Look for wreckage."

Near dusk in the well-hush that carries a whisper intact, it will hear:

"What light?"

"Moccasin Springs!"

"What of that rock for camp?"

While the bluff repeats: "Rock for camp?" there is no other sound but the *Ni-sho-dse* shifting her bulk to the current, making for shore.

The Gasconade River flows in from the southwest, for a long way parallel with the Osage. But whereas in its upper reaches the Osage enters from Kansas (as the *Marais des Cygnes*), the Gasconade is wholly Missourian. It takes its rise deep in a country of hills and springs where folk have the profile and tongue of their kin in Kentucky; where streams are hemmed by "shut-ins" and move down falls of pure porphyry, standing with "stationary blast" in many miles of silent woodland.

It is somewhat smaller than the Osage. It narrows more quickly, taking readily the characteristics of the mountain river. Yet it is the first good-sized tributary of the Missouri upward from its mouth, and it was well known in colonial days. Pine and cedar grew by it hugely so that for years timber was cut from its bank for Saint Louis. And from here came maple sugar, ponies, bear oil in skins, and cubs to be fattened in coops like hens. These were the exports of the Shawanese and Delawares who at one time

72

lived here. Their squaws took to the settlements such quantities of the sugar (*cassonade*) that some say the river itself began to be called the Cassonade—and then the Gasconade. It may be true. French place-names of the region have been uniformly unlucky. The *Ile au Bois* is called Zillaboy; the *Pomme de Terre*, Pummlytar. *Bois d'arc* is pronounced Bodark and *Boisblanc*, Wablow.

The Missouri is rising. It would prefer not to let the Gasconade out. But the smaller stream is also high. It is raining in the Ozarks as well as in Iowa. In the Ozarks slopes are steep. When water falls the water has its way. To turn out of the Missouri we are forced to use the motor. The waters literally wrestle with one another, grappling to strangle and throw down. Past a certain distance they are neither brown nor green, but a mingling as in marble. Beyond there is green only, with here and there a round mud "flower" that blossoms up in a whirlpool.

To our right, immediately, we come upon a boatyard of the U. S. E. D. Tiny, we purr along a white sidewheeler, the *Wright*; past the stern-wheelers *McIndoe* and *William Clark*; past the small boats, barrels, chests, coils, all the paraphernalia, fascinating for the landsman, of such places. At windows, rails, and doors heads appear at the sound of our buzzing. Coming down hatchways, men stop to watch, amused and admiring. A smart outfit we have. It is like entering a restaurant with a handsome woman.

Shortly beyond, on the same bank, is a colony of mongrel shanty boats, sagging happily in the mud with tin

cans and geraniums. Their inmates peer, timid or hostile;
then wave with the full length of both arms, stopping to
grin and waving again, friendly as cur hounds that jump
and lick, once convinced of your intent.

Past a bend that shuts us from the Missouri we have the
sensation of stepping under an arbor, of shutting a gate.
We are out of the wind, out of the placid neuter space
in which only a plainsman could make himself at home.
Though the arch of trees is amply high, we are not sure
we shall not strike our heads. We start at the sound of
our voices. Quietude, collected in this pocket, has stood
so long that its dross has filtered out. It is another element
present, crowding air. The *Ni-sho-dse* steams unhindered,
her chest out, like a toy boat on a mirror, the more important for her reflection. Through atmosphere which, between green arch and green stream, is also green, we look
as through a block of glass.

Below the village of Stolpe (German, need one be
told?) we find camp on a bar of gravel. Before there
can be any pitching of tents there is more serious business.
We fall to with the speed of fortunate lovers, stripping
and walking in to the clear Gasconade, soaping long after
we are clean, sinking to the ears, our fingers, legs, toes
opened rapturously, our body hair standing out still and
separate. Then we rest on the sand until dark, under stars,
by the stream that mirrors stars, so still, so black that the
scallop of our beach might be the edge of a precipice.

Because of the inconstant level of water in spring, pools
are left in the shores, whether in the hollow of an up-

turned leaf or in the mud of a basin where the stone you throw sinks with an ugly belch. There is therefore no counting of mosquitoes. They rise from a bush as from a chimney. We must sleep in the tent, and, to keep it as far as may be from the timber, we have moved to the river's edge. I notice uneasily as we turn in that the stake we have placed to note the rise is nearly under. That eloquent stake! How dully we have passed brief notes in the journals of river men:

"*On dirait que l'eau monte.*"

"Up one foot since night."

"*L'eau monte: nous avons apparence d'orage.*"

"The river seems to be rising."

Now we know what it means to see fingers of water retreating, advancing, stealthy and sucking; to hear land of the bank give way with the sound of cow dung dropping; to start up at night certain that we are cut off, with the weak knees of the somnambulist wakened in a stairway that has no rail.

A tug goes by with a barge, headed downstream. The cone of her light fumbles at the shore, fixing our bar—the danger mark. It halts as if in fright when it reaches the tent. From the pilot house, distinctly: "Well, I'll be damned!" A boatload of giggers goes by. They would have startled us had we not been familiar with them since childhood—the ball of fire to attract the fish (withering briskly the leaves that bend to it); the man in the prow, poised to hurl his spear; the plop of the end-man's pole; the voices casual as if they did not seem to be coming from a cave; the movement of the boat as if pulled on by revolving spokes of shadow.

This morning the water blows full over the site of last night's fire. It stops just short of our door. We take down the tent, pulling our equipment to higher ground, resolving to spend the day with these blond pebbles, these reflections of cedar and fern. We are gay in this clean cool. We need to relax, to dally in calm. I spend the forenoon on the beach, playing with the glasses, reversing the proportions of my world in the clouds, watching, in the amber shallows, the thrashing of minnows about a cookie I have thrown. They twist frantically in a ball, almost transparent, the thin ridges of their backs cutting through the water. Each fish in turn darts at the cake and beyond, as if it were hot. Now the picture is disturbed. On the half of the cookie still protruding from the shallows a dragonfly has lighted. He is powder blue, brighter at the head (which seems composed of eyes), and at the tail. There are two dots of the same color near the upper end of his wings, which have the shape of maple seeds and are veined with a black thread. The black thread is not a detail. Man, not Nature, places upon it less emphasis than on the passing of a planet by the moon.

The afternoon is hot. We send for beer from the village, sharing it with peasants who have come to the bar to dig gravel. They are not American farmers. They are German peasants, slow and kindly if only for the reason that they are too thick-pated to engender malice. It is strange to hear their English, fluent but ridden with such intonation that a few feet away one would swear it was German. The one of our number who knows most of the Boche goes to them, swinging his beer can, teaching them to sing: *"Schön ist die Fruehling und schön ist das Leben."* Beside him, on a log, sits one whose hair, like a fistful of straw, sticks from under a high cap, leather-visored. With his head on one side he sings, his lips protruding. At the end of each verse he smiles to right and left, not opening his lips, as if he were toothless. He places a hand on each knee, *"Ja,"* he says, *"das Leben!"*

The singers depart when the evening fish begin to leap, making circles in the reflections of willows. Dusk is chill and the night is freshened with a wind. It blows steadily inshore, forcing most of the mosquitoes to remain in the timber, so that we dare to sleep on the sand, arranging a pyramid of green elm-root fire that lays over us a hot and bitter smudge. The air has an exquisite edge, so cold that we are conscious of the hair of our inner nostril. We lie watching the stars; those that remain in place; those that give way and fall, ragged an instant before they are smoothed in flight. The man who rises in the night, rebuilding the fire, finds himself packed in a wool of mist, its moving strands so thick that of his stretched arm he sees the hand but not the elbow. Under the gray the coals glow like the heart of an opal. There is no sky and no earth beyond the circle of orange gleaming.

In the morning we break camp out of a cloud bank. Where it can be seen the water is steel, steaming as if it were almost ready to boil. The boat moves off between lines of woods that drip audibly. Branches stand out full-plumed as in tapestry, seemingly unrelated to any tree. Vales open to either side in an odd stereopticon perspective. They suck off mist from the river. They stand lush. From the tops of trees vines drop straight to the wet fronds in the mulch.

In a bend at a given point wind from the Missouri halts the mist. It pulls up short, separate bodies of it moving from side to side, crowded from behind, like the first of a herd turned by riders. We skim close to the vessels of the boatyard. We hear the clink of spoons, an order called, a footstep on the deck. A bell tinkles. While it continues, frail and querulous, we cap a kind of mound where water meets oncoming water. We are sucked out onto the Missouri. And far out in the brown, a green "flower" of the Gasconade blossoms up.

This morning, for being full of mist, has lost no brightness. Each particle of haze is sought out and handled by color. It looks substantial but it can be breathed. The wind moves it solidly in a ceiling over us, peeling it back from bluffs that stand with the bulk and finality of a seacoast. They are densely wooded, some with tonsured top; some smooth, on the sides, with fields.

By the time high noon has fried out all nuance we land, and are amused by the village of Herman. It sits at the mouth of a creek known to the French colonials and called by them the *Rivière aux Frênes*. It is in its way as foreign as French Canada—but Herman is not French.

# The Missouri

It is German to the core. German is spoken in the streets, in the stores. There is not a clean English accent within hearing. Every one is genial. Every one beyond the age of diapers has a paunch. There is everywhere about so active a ferment of animal content that even before we reach the Concert Hall Bar (with its deer-heads, its mounted fish) we are tipsy. This is not a saloon but a family club, a communal living-room, in a kind of bourgeois Vienna, minus the epaulette and spur. It is midday, yet fat mamas are resting their breasts on table edges, laughing, over beer, at the big stomach opposite. We are served excellent draught in a glass so nearly the size of an aquarium that presently we are as gummily freundlich as the rest.

The Missouri, after the shade of the Concert Hall, is vast and witheringly hot. Nodding, drowsy among the impersonal currents, we begin to look about for the night's island. It is rarely possible to camp on the mainland. On one side or the other is always a railroad. It does not often mar the scene—the engine and cars dwarfed to the shape of toys, crowing absurdly out of tunnels, scuttling like a mouse below the cliffs. At night the sound of the whistle is even pleasant over the water. It voices with uncanny thrift the excitement already compressed in the hollows of my chest. It says for me the black width of dark about the globe, the strange flowing of a world-important river, familiarly, by my cheek in the sand. With its hint of space and speed it narrows more tightly the bed I have hollowed in the beach. Yet tracks, of course, ruin camp sites, and

79

here, unfortunately, they occupy the bluff side, where the shore is high and rocky. The opposite bank is invariably bad; a mud wall surmounted by cornfields, eaten into by the current; or low woods foul from the last flood.

Yet surely there is something amiss with one who, given the choice, would refuse to live in an island. The word alone is a hall-mark of privilege, an emblem of solitude hedged formidably, not by a dead wall, but by an element so twitchingly alive that the island seems the still reduction of it—as, in the concentricity of a whirlpool, the smallest, most powerful, least active inner circle.

But, with the river so high in June, even islands fit for camp are hard to find. We must go on and on until, above the town of Washington whose lights are flicking on in the dusk, whose bridge is seen as a silver web, we find one that will do. Here the mainland makes a bay, hedged with cottonwoods, long, and lined with piles to turn the current. Upstream the sun has not yet set, a finely cut and salmon-colored ball. The whole expanse of river, hurling itself into the bend, is flushed with the same hue. It is like an arm of the sea moving out in a tide, yet with all the wild shore and the tons of water, we might be looking into a flower heart of stamen and pistil. It requires an effort of sense to remember that a false step beside the river might mean death, to recall that in this enchanted isle there is little wood to burn and not a drop for our throats except what we have from our battered jug.

This last is brought home to us by a man who lands from a rowboat, exhausted and wanting a drink. Four

hours ago he left Washington (still in sight). He under-
stands without being told that each of us will have one
third of a cup less for the cup we give him, and he will
accept only one. He lies resting in the sand, breathing
with closed lips so as not to dry his tongue. Indifferent to
the salmon bay he leaves exploration to his dog, a hound
that lurches about after its nose, as if in a limp pocket
of the hide it carried an active but uncontrolled weight.

He tells us that behind the island there enter into the
Missouri, a short distance apart, the *Rivière à Charette*
and the *Rivière à Tuque*. Inland between the mouths is
Marthasville, descendant of Old Charette village, to
which came, seeking new wilderness, one Daniel Boone.
Near by is the house in which he died. In the region
between here and the *Femme Osage*, he had his last
homes. It was from here that he set out, an old man
attended by one nigger, to hunt on the *Rivière Bourbeuse:*
from here that he left to visit the Yellowstone!

We quiet down to sleep, our three beds hollowed in the
sand which is loose as salt. The top of our covering is soon
soaked with dew. There is dark and the firefly wink of
navigation lights. Tonight the moon passes north of Ju-
piter so that they are near together when they rise, the
planet brave as a young stallion that has galloped out
to see. I hear the sigh of water that collects, hesitates
and flows more rapidly; the whimper of a loose log
caught in the piles. Then no more until the sun wakes me
to a morning so vast that visible earth is one line, an un-
important flatness. Granted this observation as from a

point in space, we can see the weather of a whole section
of globe. Above us is sun and calm of summer cloud. In
five separate places about us we see rain. It hangs in lines
that crisscross and look taut. Under them gutters are
awash, the cattle turn their backs and banks erode.

We set out in a chorus of pensive Sunday bells that call
and answer. Briefly we stop at the town of Washington,
torpid in its Sabbath. There the temperature is 98. On the
river it must be more. In the canoe lies my body and I,
curiously, with it. Its whole length seems not a part of
me, like a leg that has "gone to sleep." Glowing, it keeps
its shape, yet by a process resembling petrifaction its atoms
one by one have been replaced with particles of light.

The sheet of water flowing, the heat and space, the
spray, the breast of swell, the changing changeless crest
of wavelets all combine to cancel sense of time and place.
Where did we camp the night before last? Was it there
that the ball-eyed frog leaped by the fire, its tongue flashing at the ants that ran from the flame? Was it there
that we heard the hounds in the night, baying from the
mainland? Was it there that we met the old nigger skin-
ning a spoonbill cat? Was it there, or somewhere else,
that we found the king-snake in midstream, lifted and
dropped by the water, his tongue fanning briskly? Since
time and longitude have lost their sense it is by such
benchmarks that we fix position. Reckoning is halted at a
break in the perimeter, a gap through which there blows
a wind from what has been and what will be. Place is

always a green island crowned with swallows. Time whirls off at a tangent, like a hat dropped in this current that carries us so fast.

Past Du Bois Creek. Past Saint Albans. Past the mouth of the *Rivière à la Femme Osage*. Then, seeing what we take to the village of Hamburg, we land, seeking shade and cold beer. There is no beer, but shade in plenty and with it a quiet broken by the rattle of cottonwood leaves. Our steps resound as we move among the empty buildings. Hamburg is deserted. It has moved from the railroad a mile away to the "slab," where there is cheap trucking, where there is always something doing. The railroads have their ruins now, as the seamboats had.

This morning we are soon in sight of the bridges of Saint Charles, which has little to show of its past as the *Saint Charles des Petites Côtes* of the French. There is, as in Quebec, a respectable upper town and a richly dis-reputable-looking *basseville*. We tie up among the scanty gardens of the shanty-boat folk, buy our supplies quickly, and leave. The sidewalks are hard under our moccasins, the shops and dwellings repulsive to our eye. The citizens, for a bathroom and electric light, have given their liberty too easily. We return their look of suspicion, in fury pull-ing out a roll of bills before a grocer who states, before he serves, that terms are cash. He is a degenerate whose instep is not supported by the cool sand; who never walks from the tent in the morning not remembering dress, naked among the willows that shower dew on his skin, in the chill air that moves unhindered over throat and rib, under the crotch and down the thigh. Homesick for space, we put out as soon as we can, under a flight of herons which have like us, and for the same reason, chosen the far shore.

Below town in a bend we sight the *General McIndoe*, headed upstream. Later these meetings will make a joyous diversion. For the moment our hearts are in our throats. This is the first time the *Ni-sho-dse* has been forced to carry us through the wake of a steamer. We slow our pace, turning this way and that, avoiding the swift water that pours off the jetties, until the *McIndoe's* course is plain. She runs by smartly, her red wheel veiled in mist, throwing up, for a hundred yards behind, uniform mounds of water, curled at the top like conventional waves in drawing. Soon the roll reaches us, forcing us to turn into it, sending our prow far out of water, bringing us down with a belly-slap, stinging us with a sleet of spray. For a quarter of a mile the whole river is agitated.

Well satisfied with ourselves, we move on to camp in an island opposite *La Charbonnière*. Here at one time in the hill was visible a seam of coal. Lewis and Clark noted it, translating the name Coal Hill. Pike thought it would "afford sufficient fuel for all of Louisiana." Here the French Trappists landed, bound inland for Saint Ferdinand de Florissant. Here came ashore Mother Duchesne and her nuns, the lot of them busy with their cow; not one dreaming of canonization. And here in 1817 the steamer *Western Engineer* put in, having on board Major

Long and the men of his expedition to the Yellowstone. There is not now (nor has there been for long) any coal in sight. If the seam is there it has slipped beneath the river.

This last of our islands in the Missouri is large enough that we must look sharply to follow our own tracks when we have strayed from camp. It is formed entirely of sand, moulded to the shapes in which the water left it, in rolls, in ridges, in areas ribbed like the bony mouth of fish, dunes designed as if by wind. There are thickets of sycamore, growths of willow so dense that a pencil could not be inserted between their trunks; clearings grown with a wiry grass, with cocklebur and sunflower. Through all of this is traced the furious path of flood streams, dry and piled with wreckage, having at intervals circles scooped out like salt licks, cracked and brittle, where water stood before it evaporated.

Outward from camp the shelved sand drops to a beach, to the wet where crows prance and bow to each other. There are at the water's edge a dead turtle, buckeyes and acorns, colored stones fresh washed, a fish's head and skin with heron tracks about. Fireflies move among the stems of the tall grass. Beyond them the river flows from between dark islands, salmon and lavender, olive restless with silver. We are not many miles from its mouth. It flows with an extra fullness, with the level speed of a billiard ball. The panorama upstream and down is vast, but there are clouds to dwarf it; clouds with the shape and color of sea anemone, the highest spreading "button" moving up into the last light.

Knowing what is in store for us we leave, in the morning, with less than our usual carelessness. Without admitting it to one another, we sit falsely "at ease," like pioneers entering the Indian country.

We are diverted for an instant by the Lewis and Clark Bridge and Bellefontaine. In this region, in 1768, the Spanish built their Fort Prince Charles. In 1805 it was the site of the first American military post in Louisiana. Beck, in 1817, notes that it had a palisade large enough to admit 3000 men. In 1837 (so rapid was the march of the frontier) Wetmore trumpets importantly: "The barracks have crumbled to dust and the ploughshare has passed over the promenade of the sentinel." Before the Americans or the Spanish, the French had known the place. The stream that falls to the Missouri here they called variously *La Rivière à la Belle Fontaine* or *La Rivière à la Fontaine aux Biches;* both with reference to a spring since destroyed by the encroachments of the river. The Spaniards called it Ferdinand; the Americans, Clearwater.

Meanwhile our hearts tighten. The mileage sinks towards zero. The river widens and is slow, spreading in a marsh. There is very nearly perfect quiet; a little humming of water only, of wind and of blood in our ears. Surely if we were brought here blindfolded we should know that we were headed for something great and not far distant. We should gather ourselves as one who stands, foot lifted, nearly treading on a snake. Though the banks are low and the scene has no great feature to make it dramatic, the Missouri is nowhere so respectable. It is deep and serene, the river that quarried so lately, and strove. With a gesture unhurried and simple because it is great, the West moves out to meet the North in a field of water with limits not easy to fix from the floor of a canoe. There is not the roaring that caused Marquette to raise his head, but a hush that sucks all to it, muffling as the silence of uncharted caves. There is no sign, even today, of man and his genial works. Migrant Siouans divided here. Joliet passed. Lewis and Clark turned in. But none of them count. This joining is old as the swoop of hawks is old, and the print of fern in coal. It is anterior to history and will go on after, remote as archipelagoes upon the moon.

We cross easily the quiet water between the left point and the meeting of the streams, moving forward onto the Mississippi. We know geography better, but we feel as the explorers did, entering from the east tributaries. So great is our conviction that we have *come out at something,* that we have an echo of their surprise to find not a blue Gulf of California nor a shore of Yucatan—not the end— but the heart only, of this amazing land. We know their dismay, and yet their glee that for a time they may go on, under stars they have come to know, toward the unknown sea.

# IV

# THE MISSISSIPPI

## IV

# The Mississippi

THE *Ni-sho-dse* for an instant is stationary. She is even swept back a little. It is as if we lay in a groove of something solid. Looking overboard at the striped flowing we have the same impression as when, in a sidetracked local, we are passed by an express: it is we who seem to be moving, not the river. Then, with motor on full, halted, shaken by white caps and allowed to go on, we make obliquely for the eastern shore where we may head due north in quiet water.

We meet the *Tom Sawyer*, southbound from Wood River, and take her swell. We pass the Chippewa Light, and turn out for the docks of a great oil company: here there are eight or ten boats from New Orleans, from Cincinnati, Louisville and Memphis; vessels which will pass us frequently, whose faces we shall come to know.

We poke into the mouth of Wood River. It is polluted by the industries of a town near by, but we wish to see it particularly. It is connected in history with a spot we have just passed—the site of La Charette on the Missouri. Once in the winter of 1803 two strangers knocked there at

91

the cabin of Daniel Boone. One, after all, was not a stranger: Boone had known him as a child in Kentucky. His name was William Clark and that of his gentler companion, Meriwether Lewis. They meant to head an expedition up the unmapped Missouri in the spring and, meanwhile, wished to winter with Boone. The imagination is free to play about this meeting, this moment when the live energy of fate gathers visibly in a given spot, as under a magnifying lens light can be drawn to one hot point. Boone, from the Yadkin, from the Cumberland Gap, from the Clinch and the Holston, from the Bloody Ground, meets with Lewis and Clark the sons of the men who had fought at Point Pleasant and King's Mountain. The boys are going to the Pacific. Frontier is imposed over frontier, as the shadow of a planet moving intercepts the moon.

Permission to camp with Boone was refused by the Spaniards. Obliged to return to American soil, the men came here where we are, at the mouth of Wood River. They holed up until the floes thinned out and crests of willows took the henna tinge of early spring.

Issuing again to the Mississippi we are caught close to shore by the *Franklin Roosevelt* and in the barrage of waves are busy, so that time goes by before we look up to find that the dam and bridges of Alton have moved into sight; the chimneys and spires of a city on the hills. There we go to land in the mud. It smells of oil and fish and excrement. Upstream the whole river is shut off by a dam.

# The Mississippi

It was put there, surely, for its usefulness; yet it has a lively æsthetic appeal. Its honest monster bulk, its clean planes that take the light as in an etching, make as fine a sight as the aqueduct of Nîmes.

We are told (rightly or not we have wondered since) that, because a gate of the dam is open, we must attempt to pass through it before asking to use the lock. The signal man wigwags: clear ahead. We move forward then, but with lower hearts at every foot we gain. Already we see water rushing, and hear an angry hum. Inch by inch we split the current, make the entrance of the gate, and go in. The boat is almost stopped. She sways and is righted. She pitches and ships a little water. She is hemmed with writhing foam, spun so fine that it does not seem wet. The motor is on full blast but we do not hear it. One to another we yell advice but no sound seems to come from the open mouth. We creep to the far end of the tunnel—and then no farther. Before us water stands in muscles three feet high, motionless as in a carving. There is no more power to give. We are halted, wobbling like a ball on the crest of a fountain. If we cannot go forward then we must retreat, but backwards, in a straight line. Diversion of an inch to either side will crack us up against the wall. Our bodies will be spat out at the piers of the bridge below. How the manœuvre was executed the pilot knows, perhaps, and God. And the same can tell, no doubt, if it is solely with water of the river that our pants were wet as we are let into the lock reserved for small boats. We call out facts required by an official and slip out the small crack in the great door, embarrassed that this mechanism should be called to work for us.

After such tension our gaiety takes no thought but for itself. We sit with a carton of beer bottles on the town landing between an office of the Eagle Packet Company and a fish market. From under the porch of the market comes a litter of kittens. Their feet are not so light on the sand as ours.

Facing the sun near sunset we take out, meeting around the first bend the *Katie Lyons* of Pittsburgh. The waves she sends are colored to the bottom of their troughs, as if the flush were not laid on without but rose from glowing depth. At the same time, to the right, we have the Piasa Bluff. On it is painted something intended to suggest the original demons the Indians put there. They were already dim when Saint Côme sailed by in 1698. And Marquette's sketch is lost. Therefore the likeness is in doubt. But the figure is sobering nonetheless: it recalls that the bluff, for two hundred and sixty-seven years, has seen us whites go by.

To its very mouth the Missouri keeps an Indian tang, a wild, unruly Western way. Here above the junction the Mississippi is full-lipped, and sweet; swift but orderly in its speed; softer, more feminine than the Missouri. At Saint Louis it is already Southern and has the Southern look it will not lose until it meets the sea. Up here it is Northern—Northern already of the North of lakes and silence, of evergreens and the cleft-heart track of deer beneath the moon. At this point where we are it has reached the deciduous woods, but it is still a thing whose home is with clean needles and with cones.

Illinois stands in gray palisades. Missouri is low and green. Between them we steer through the sunset water, rising so that we can look down about us; sinking to rise again, behind us a trail of bubbles, oyster-colored over the orange that begins to catch the lavender of dusk. When clefts begin to hold mist and the peninsulas that were green ahead go black, we reach an island. It is flat and timbered at its heart so densely that dark is always gathered there. It is moist and pungent with leaf-rot. Under trees whose boughs stand flat from the trunk above our heads we put the tent. And there we sleep until we are wakened by the pulse of a steamer; by the thrust of her light against the shore—a sharp cone in which the mist revolves. From the second deck it darts out full and snaps off. But the picture it lit remains on our eyes—the elms standing from earth like the dirt of explosions, in the split second when it has ceased to rise and has not spread to fall.

In the morning we leave on a river minutely covered with wavelets. Each flashes as its point finds the light. Each, as it whips to full length, detaches a few drops that, multiplied by thousands, give the whole blue stream a rhinestone glitter. There is cold wind to shrink our scalps, to keep hair in our eyes as we try to look up at the "summer gulls" that follow us. The pilot is singing at his post. With wind and spray the notes of Mozart jug by, winking out. Here where the unchristian whine of savages or Creole boatmen's tunes would be at home the song is absurdly inappropriate. It comes like the call of a land-bird lost over water, giving out over foam what naturally comes from under leaves. It stings with the nostalgia an eighteenth-century gentleman might have felt here in his pirogue on the Mississippi—he remembering a marquise at home; her *mouches*, her edited curls, her breasts laced by a velvet string.

As the surface grows more choppy, we make for the Missouri shore, putting between us and the palisades the breadth of river. The wall of willows beside us is solid. At our shoulders and above our heads are uncounted red-wings and cardinals. Before us the boughs "give" with the weight of herons, disengaging themselves in fright. Having no beach from which to take off they pitch forward and back an instant, until with balance of chapped leg and incredible neck they can settle into flight.

Entering behind an island we come to the landing of the Portage des Sioux, and walk a muddy road to the village. There is a post-office—with the name of the town over its door in the lettering of handbills of 1860—and a scattering of houses; some very pleasant, a few old and of architecture inspired by the Creole. This settlement was founded by François Saucier, who had been in command of Fort Massac on the Ohio when it was surrendered to the English. He came to Louisiana and, probably as early as 1767, had a plantation on this ground. In 1799 he founded the village to offset the influence of Americans who were thought to be building a military post "at the place called Piasa."

But long before plantation or village the locality had its name. In the days when they still dwelt on the lower Missouri, the Missouri Indians, hearing that the Sioux were headed down the Mississippi to attack them, ambushed themselves at the mouth of their river. But the Sioux, landing at the spot called ever since the Portage des Sioux, pulled their canoes over the narrow tongue of land that divides the two streams and attacked from behind. The peninsula they crossed is subject to inundation. It is flat and sown with "lakes" such as the *Marais Croché* and the *Marais Espagnol,* which occupy fragments of old river bed. It is soggy and grown so densely with willows that one who enters hacks his way. Thus, almost within sight of a large city, the place has kept a look elaborately wild, as on the day the Sioux came down gesticulating, secret and exuberant, choosing the portage.

Upward from this point there is a chain of islands. Between them and the Missouri shore one may ride in a channel less swift than the main stream. They are finger islands long and slender, hung with the elms. Over these and the water move the shadows of cloud shapes. Now the islands stand dark and the river lies in a chasm of light. Now the river flows a dull pewter and the islands are set off, brilliantly green, exactly hemmed by water and by shade.

We come into the main channel again, a trifle below

the mouth of the Illinois. Now we learn that while we were moseying in shelter, things were happening in the world outside. A squall has been romping over the Mississippi. Downstream about a mile the horizon is still smoky with rain. The moist heat of afternoon has been rent with cold. The air is washed. And the water whips like flame where the Mississippi is butted in the flank by the Illinois with its load from the Iroquois, the Kankakee, the Des Plaines, the Fox and the Sangamon.

There is a crossing before us of a mile and a quarter—and more, since we are headed for Grafton in the mouth of the Illinois. The choppiness ends in a bed of waves. Their crests snap in our face matting our hair, stinging our cheeks, landing water on the nape of our neck, in our lap, as if it had been aimed there from a bucket. Our prow, held strictly to the attack, rises and slaps down in a hard "V" of spray. Between shocks the whole boat shakes like a wet dog. Exposed to air the propeller whangs angrily: submerged again and on an upward slope it sends us forward with the jerk of a rope gone taut. In the midst of this we forget that time has gone by to refuel the motor. We do not remember until we are safe in haven at Grafton. There, finding barely a moisture in the tank, we sweat with belated excitement, seeing how near we have been to making a chore for Christopher.

The Illinois is broad, and so steady, so quiet that any upstream traveller experiences the relief that Marquette felt when, sick in soul and body, he turned to it in 1673.

# The Mississippi

For a certain distance about the mouth the left shore is low and swampy: it is a thin sliver of land holding the Illinois from the Mississippi. The right bank has a range of rolling hills a short way back, some wooded, some cleared for farms.

As we pass the Deer Plain Ferry, preparing to enter Cherokee Bend, rain begins. A few drops, fat and deliberate, as if they dripped from the end of a wet towel. They fall like marbles into the river, each sending up a silver twig of water where it lit. We land, hurriedly, to pitch the tent in a narrow margin between the sand of the beach and a field of corn. The sky goes black. Breakers of ink white capped with foam bite at the bank. A gale howls off the prairies to the east, raking the hills. Willows crouch, revolve and leap: the corn blades stand rigid from the stalk. If we had not the weight of our bodies and baggage in the middle of the floor, the tent would roll like a newspaper over the field. Even so anchored it strains and lifts its corners in the wind, so that we are in the lap of a hammock.

The force passes, crossing the deltas of the Illinois, the Missouri; playing havoc (so we hear later) with telephone poles and window glass in Saint Louis. We have a cold meal in the tent, by flashlight, and lie the night tightly buttoned behind the flaps. Outside a whining "February" wind drowns the breakers that crash almost within reach, so that we do not hear them, but feel their tremors in our shoulders and hips. Actually we have a good ten feet between us and their closest impact. This we forget as we wake uneasily in the dark. Something primitive within us, shamed by reason, is frantic because it is enclosed—something that would step out, braving anything for a chance to fight.

This morning, after the storm, the base of the tent, the foot of trees, the sides of the boat, are splattered with earth driven against them. Rocks and sticks of the beach lie elevated a little on the sand that was under them when rain beat down the sand about them. The sky is cold and bruised. Everything is still, dripping. The water is disturbed, but with a swell as of long sighs that urge the lung to full expansion, held an instant with diaphragm trembling.

As we are shaving dry wood from the heart of a log, the *Comanche* of Peoria eases by. Her superstructure is clear in the rain-washed air. From her stacks lie out behind two trails of smoke, billowing but flat and exact, as if they were cut with scissors from black paper. She lets herself about the bend, strangely narrow when she has turned toward us only her butt-end; the tall wheel throwing water from blade to blade, lathering foam. Her wake rolls up the beach, setting our coffee cups afloat.

Today, with the wind so high and cold, with the sky so dark, we have no heart for travel. Morning goes by in a search for our scattered equipment. Aimless dawdling takes the afternoon. Night lightens our hearts with the clear stars of good weather, and with chill to keep down mosquitoes. Our windblown fire gives the uneven light of a lamp held up out of doors. The water uncurls with fastidious precision at our toes. On spread ponchos we watch from sight the moving red and green of a plane among the stars. In that jewelled beetle a man sits at the controls. He has like me a watch on his wrist, a filling in his tooth, hair on his legs. Looking up at his lights that go with the slide of raindrops, but laterally, across the sky, finding his little humanness in the black, I sense the isolation of my predecessors here. La Salle, tough as he was in that winter of search for his lost companions, may well have felt this hesitancy as at a brink.

At daylight we leave, in and out of troughs that are deep but gentle. All morning we have a sibilant prow and a champagne wake, its bubbles visible still on the crests of the swell behind. Once clear of Cherokee Bend the water is quieter. We burrow through a region which, if the immediate banks are to be trusted, is a wilderness of cottonwood and willow. For us, after the Missouri, after the Mississippi, the Illinois is lulling and oppressive. It continues a little more and a little less than a quarter of a mile wide, deep and green and steady. But, in colonial days, this very monotony was its virtue. It had a portage of scarcely a mile over level ground to Lake Michigan; a gentle current; no rapids, shoals or falls. Its Indians were for the most part friendly. It was the best road to Canada.

About twenty miles from its mouth it widens appreciably for a time. Closing a long perspective, the white buildings of Hardin cast reflections indistinguishable from those of the limestone hills. We poke on past the village into the green again, past a rare house, past an occasional shell fisherman, his boat bordered with brails like an old surrey.

At night, some miles below the first dam, we find an acceptable island. The few lanky cottonwoods at its edge give way to honest forest trees within—oak and elm and giant pecan. It was doubtless along about here that the French descending from Canada began to discover the "exotic" pecan, the pawpaw and the persimmon. In an eighteenth-century book—Charlevoix, perhaps—I remember a drawing of a persimmon of the Illinois; leaf overlapping leaf formally as if it were laurel about the head of Cæsar; the fruit set brightly as in holly; and hanging from a limb, exquisitely limp, a *rat de bois* (an opossum), with a look of good-natured deceit.

Under the inland trees there is an all but impenetrable growth of hawthorn, whose lowest branches flatten at a certain height, shutting away the light. The ground beneath is even as a board, covered thickly with violets. What a sight in spring—a sifting of white petals on the green and purple floor! What wonder that eighteenth-century humanitarians seized upon descriptions sent home by travellers; imagining here a race of Earth Children shapely and brown, filling cradles of bark with moss for their young to swing from a flowering bough!

In the center of the island we place the tent where the land is cleared except for the pecans. The site is so flat and the island so narrow that we can see water flowing to either side, flat also, and very green. The mainland behind shows a bluff that breaks into bare stone above its woods. In the interval between its foot and our grove the air is densely blue, blue with the goblin blue of Ozark springs. Through its mist three deer-eyed Jerseys walk to have us scratch their brows.

Offshore a buoy marks the channel, wallowing and lolling in a dance like giants in the parade at Nice. A red-and-yellow tug rounds the island opposite and disappears, her tow-knees nibbling foam. Downstream comes a steamer with a long load of barges. She moves into the space between our island and the next, huge and, beyond belief, incongruous. It is as if you should glance up to see a locomotive in the door of your music room. Suddenly the quiet is rent by the bellow of a steam whistle so loud that it jars the roots of our hair from their hold in the scalp. Is it a warning to an approaching boat? An accidental flatulence? Neither. From the pilot house an arm is waving. And through the silence falling back we hear a simple: "Hah yuh, boys?" We have been told good night.

Dusk grows thick. The bright silver flowing to either hand is all we see—that and the fireflies that flick off as we note their position. It is the moment when owls begin; when doves have not left off; and when mosquitoes are not as bad as they will be. Before the tent we talk, resolving to leave the Illinois. Let it ride on fat and calm from the North, out of the prairies of the buffalo, of the Peorias, the Cahokias, the Kaskaskias; of the French and the English and the Yankees. Down from Tonti's Starved Rock and the Fort Crêve Cœur. Down from the Sangamon where Lincoln piloted his steamer. Ourselves, we are going South. Tomorrow in stillness and cold we shall go down again to Cherokee Bend feeling in outstretched arms, holding the paddle, the impulse and the stroke's gain; seeing the prow dip and foam rise. And the morning after, moving through the green gate of the Illinois, we shall ride out on the musical bright tons of the Mississippi milling and shifting with great bulk and great ease. Currents will dovetail, strong over weak, hissing as on a blade of shallows. Breasts of swell will start up bundled as sheaves are shown in art, but silver-capped, but living, sending their beauty all to the quick crest. So, passing under the cliffs the explorers called the "ruined castles," threading islands that keep their silence before us, we shall land once more on the shore of the pitching field where Missouri and Mississippi meet.

From a camp in the thickets and sand of the Missouri's lower lip we move into a southeast wind. The water, alternating quickly from slate to crystal in the changing bright and dark of the sky, is deeply pocked, flagged everywhere with white caps. We sight the first of the Saint Louis bridges, the Chain of Rocks; then the bulk of Cabaret Island. We should camp here on the tip of the island if we were wise; or, if we continue, we should take the less frequented Illinois shore, not the Missouri. Innocently we take the wrong way. And evidence of our error is heaped upon us instantly by waves. There is obviously at all times a very pretty current between the end of the island and the Missouri bank. Now, this water, normally swift to the south, is checked by a wind from the south. It stands, unwilling, in mounds that sway like bears, and with the surprising speed of bears, lunging smartly. Since our great and simple idea is to remain prow-and-stern with the force and never to be taken broadside by it, we are in a bad way. Our course stems necessarily from the safe straight line. We are sent up in the air and brought down with a jar which we feel in the bones of our teeth —and this so often that we feel safe when we arrive at the shore, threatened only by bridge piers, docks and moving steamers.

On such days we are accustomed to find a margin of quieter water near the bank, where with caution we may go our way. Today, precisely, the margin is swallowed by a big port. The river ahead is hemmed by the metropolitan districts of Saint Louis on the one hand and East Saint Louis on the other. We are forced to the tumult of midstream, and back again when we see that it is a matter of minutes before we are overturned.

Though the day is young it ends for us when a wave drives us full at the flank of the *S.S. Minnesota*. It spends its force so that we do not crash, but ease slowly to the great deck, squeezing suds of dirty foam from its side into our laps. This time the lesson is clear. Poling along the *Minnesota* we crawl under her stern into a little bay left between the bank and her portside. It is not a lovely refuge. Down from the high shore are strewn millions of tin cans. Rats peer and run. But we are safe, and we have

a welcome from the crew. They tell us that the river will
be quiet tonight; that on days of such wind all small craft
are grounded here. We must be patient. No dispensation
can be made for us.

We do not expect it. But, meanwhile, there is a day
on our hands. Leaving one man alternately to guard our
equipment, we visit the waterfront. A bum who is standing
in the door of a mission calls out: "Hey boys! Hey youse!
Wheh youse boys frum?" He offers us a testament with
the words of Christ in red. A woman picking her teeth
at a window says: "Like to come in, honey?" And she
grins when we refuse. "Yah, y'ain't got time!" A bar-
keep, before he will serve us beer, asks to see our money.
Beside his other customers we are black as coons. They are
men from a flour mill. They wear white caps and overalls.
Their faces and hands are blue.

Near by there is a shanty town as large as a village.
There are "streets" of "houses" built of refuse. Eyes glare
at us from the windows like the eyes of owls in a hole.
We are beset by children, product of the sole joy of this
place. "Gimme nickel, mister? Gimme nickel?" The dress
is torn and it is all she wears, so that her tragic little sex
is plain to all. The baby brother stumbles to his knees.
Before he gets up he puts in his mouth something he has
found in the gutter. A voice from somewhere shrills: "Git
in hyar, you!"

When we return to the boat the *Minnesota* is gone,
leaving us exposed. Night will come soon and the wind
has not died as predicted. A policeman stopping to ex-

amine the *Ni-sho-dse* advises us not to move. A tramp
beside him agrees, adding that the wind sometimes lasts
three or four days. He points to a tug moving upstream.
The water strikes her bow, streaming over the pane of
the pilot house. For all that we will not pass the night
where the rats of shanty town may draw their filthy tails
across our throats.

We push off, using all our little power, heading upstream and across, swallowed at once in troughs four feet
deep. We descend their sides at an angle. The lining of
my stomach collapses helplessly when I turn and realize
that I am looking *up* at the pilot. On the upward slope
the prow fries in foam: before the water breaks over at
us it bulges like the fat of a man's neck above the collar.
On a crest we crane to see, a half mile back, the little
group about the policeman. They are watching with greed
and with a hope they would not avow.

In shallow water finally, we leap out to pull the boat
ashore where, between the river and the hell of East
Saint Louis, there is a little greenery. Here we would stay
until first light, when the water will be quieter and the
big boats will not yet be out. But we are roughly sent off
by a po' white. He ain't lettin' *no*body on this land.

Two hundred feet below I spot a nigger fishing from
a point. Beyond, there is ugly water boiling. This is our
last chance. "Uncle," I shout, "you'll have to move over.
I'm bringing you some gentlemen to spend the night!"
There is a pause. If he's a city nigger it won't work: and

in East Saint Louis no sober man would start a fight. He eyes me shrewdly for a moment. Then he cackles. He ain' heard no tawk lak that since he left home. I learn with relief that home is Alabama. "Uncle," I can tell him honestly, "my great-grandfather was born in Talledega!" Lawd God, that's a close tie now! Sho we can stay. We look lak right nice boys. Mebbe we've even got a little tobacco about us. Sure now that he is a natural nigger, I thrust cigarettes upon him and turn to unpack the little we shall need—Uncle explaining the while that a body can tell I've been raised with black folks and that he has a good gun he'd be proud to leave with me, case that air shanty white should try to drive me off.

The sun drops like an angry squid, casting color through the smoke. Above the tossing water the full profile of Saint Louis rises. The tiny silhouettes of freights creep over bridges with restless bells. Six adult herons pass at different levels: below them are twenty-six white young ones, scattered with the flutter of paper thrown from a window. They gather to one cluster and rise high over a boat that pulls from shore.

Night falls on this strangest of strange camps. Our friends will swear that we lie when we say we have camped in East Saint Louis. Yet, in simple truth, it is just behind us, with stockyards, gangsters, whores. Opposite, the tiered lights of Saint Louis over the rats; over the tin cans. Nevertheless, when I make my bed in the canoe, I lie rocked in shallows, shoved by the spent waves as by a bedfellow; through a pattern of willow over me I see the horn of a young moon; a hawk comes down holding himself to one line—I do not think he can see me but when I stir he veers; after him comes an owl in blunt plush flight. And at the first hint of light a heron ends his downward drop at my shoulder. He begins to walk along the sand tall and casual as if he were saying to himself: "Hum diddy hum diddy hum." His wings scoop out wide in surprise as I sit upright.

We set out with no breakfast at four o'clock. The rising wind still holds from the south. Skyscrapers stand sleeping hugely in the gilt mist, pitiful and stupid as any bully when slumber halts his blustering. We keep to the Illinois side in water relatively still, passing under Ead's Bridge, once a world-wonder, the admiration of Walt Whitman who came to stand on it. Under it lies the Old Levee, sloping, paved with sugar-loaf blocks, backed by the warehouses of the fur-trade days, capped by the spire of the French Cathedral, by the Roman dome of the Old Courthouse. This Saint Louis stands as it is shown in engravings and in woodblocks, eloquently small. The modern city rises behind and around it as bark is disturbed about a scar. It is from here however that the rest radiates. It is this that proclaims Saint Louis to be not a boom town hiccoughing in its surfeit, but a deep-rooted city with a tart old beldame for its ma. Here Chouteau landed in 1764, under orders from Laclède. Here lived the canny Lisa, first to sense the meaning of the voyage of Lewis and Clark: from here, with the Chouteaus, he directed the systematic slaughter of the plains animals. Here the exiled pirates of Lafitte came hiding. Under the spire of *Saint Louis de France* gathered the congregation, literally Catholic, of Frenchman and Spaniard, Irishman, nigger, and converted Indian; the *coureur de bois* out of the West, tipsy and blinking at the lights; the keel-boat crew, and Mandan chieftains in on a mission—all of them summoned by the bell, *Pierre-Joseph-Félicité*, gift to the church of Madame de Piernas de Portneuf. At the Courthouse men said good-by to the barrel-ribbed "schooners" headed out to the sage, to the alkali, to the bright bones. And there they went to examine the pectoral muscles, the biceps of a "prime field hand"; the wrists and ankles of a good brood wench. The slave market was held on the steps. The Old Levee was French convent-bred, and since those days she has seen a lot. But she has had good fiber and has stood up with spirit. Today she has the look of one of whom, chuckling, you say: "The damned old rascal!"

Far on below the city sprawls. The mouth of the *Rivière des Pères* is hidden: the site on its banks where there stood a first settlement, antedating that of 1764 by fifty-eight years, is not distinguishable from any other mile of brick. Nor is there any boundary to mark the old village of Carondolet, once a separate settlement where one night a steamer stopped with General Lafayette; the Creoles brought him crystals from the mines, and a little fawn with its legs bent under it.

So, on the Illinois side, there was no way to isolate from

110

East Saint Louis the village of Notre Dame des Cahokias.
With Kaskaskia it was the first settlement in these parts.
It has a few old houses yet, and an eighteenth-century
church. In that village Pontiac was killed in 1764. And
there, before Indians or French, lived an unknown race
which left a scattering of mounds that dot the countryside
with their old backs.

When finally the city begins to peter out the bluffs jut
from the Missouri side. And southward for many miles
greatest beauty is found on the right bank, as it was on
the left above the mouth of the Missouri.

We ride a high swell wrinkled finely by wind, like a
section of human skin under a glass. To avoid the tumble
of midstream we steer shoreward along a jetty, then down
to the next jetty and out again. So until we come to Jefferson Barracks, since territorial days an important post.
It has seen many a famous man. Among others, Robert
Lee. And Jefferson Davis stopped here with his prisoner,
Black Hawk, taking him afterwards to Fortress Monroe.
To us, swinging our feet from a wall, the soldiers drilling
in their quad seem repulsively martinetish. The best they
can give us is the roll of their snares, the gold of their
bugle in the wood. Over the water with nothing in sight
that might not have been there in 1800, those sounds
have their rightful place. They have accompanied armies
along these shores before—the corps of regulars; the handful of Long Knives disdainful and out of step; with a
scattering of friendly Indians.

## Where the Rivers Meet

Out of the noon glare of the Mississippi we turn into the mouth of the Maramec, into a green tunnel where the *Ni-sho-dse* moves like a quail in clean stubble. This stream takes its rise in the Ozarks, coming east some two hundred miles through land important in the history of the colony. Its name has been made *Miaramigoua, Miarameg, Marameg, Maramec* and *Merrimac*. It must have come from an Indian word like the Chippewa *man-um-aig* (catfish). The French inclined to Maramec though sometimes, translating, they call it the *Rivière à la Barbue* (Catfish River). A Jesuit, writing in 1700, speaks of a lead mine on its banks; and D'Iberville, requesting privileges in the region (1702), words his petition so as to imply that mining had begun sometime back. Around 1719 the stream saw a settlement of the King's miners, who came bringing blacks from Saint Domingue, the first slaves of *La Haute Louisiane*. It was this presence of lead (and hope of silver) that brought the French in numbers from the east bank of the Mississippi where they had settled first.

Having lunched in comfort and cool, in light which seems to pass through tight green silk, we drop back to the Mississippi.

Below the mouth of the Missouri the Mississippi naturally has lost its clarity. But its size is so great that in the glittering heat of afternoon it is nonetheless blue; blue of the sort women call "baby blue," flecked with gold and half moons of foam from the white caps. I lie on the back of my neck among the hot leather cushions, watching through my lashes the swell that rolls into hummocks. Wrenched by a movement from beneath, they snap like wet blankets, sending off separate drops that catch the light. Sometimes the snap breaks full against our gunwale, spreading a fine dust, shot with colors of the rainbow, that settles invisible on my face, tickling as it dries.

Opposite tiny Kimmswick, whose inhabitants complain of its chief charm—green and leaf-smothered torpor—we tie up in a bay, ourselves quite willing to yield to sloth. Here we have the bowl of a sand beach, shut off from behind by a tangle of logs which the river has dropped, many so large that they would have to be moved with a derrick. Pushing over a smaller one that protrudes into our shade, we uncover a nest, deep enough to receive a hen egg, and pure white because it is made of new cotton from the cottonwood tree. Out of it run two mice, leaping with clean pink feet, their eyes like bits of broken bead. All afternoon and evening, on the even bowl-side of the beach, there is the pound of incoming water. It curls forward, drops under its own weight, and pushes up the sand until it is as thin as a blade, its bubbles bursting. Over the slide it has made it rolls up and pulls back fine grains of quartz; along the scallops of its farthest reach it deposits the heaviest of these, in lines that crisscross like the trail of worms. These fragile tracings, and the mice, within yards—within inches—of the Mississippi.

At sundown I stretch out to bed in the canoe. It is caught in the young willows which are half submerged, palsied by the movement of water. As if my own spine were the axle on which it might revolve completely, it rocks from side to side. The wind is soft. Occasionally it mews in the stems of the willows. It pushes the water to a sibilant fold which strikes the stern of the canoe obliquely, recording delicately in my flesh the minute bursting of bubbles until my flesh is less a length of meat and pinkish bone than an effect, also, of the river dusk. I am so merged with willow and water that ducks fly over me unperturbed, their necks outstretched, limp feet drawn to the breast. With brisk efficient flight, their wings at a distance setting a hummingbird blur beside their bodies, they make over the mile of twilight water, quiet now, and so flat that it looks concave.

Morning is hot already before the mist is gone. Early though we leave we are in for a sizzling. Before we are under weigh an hour we begin looking for shelter. Past miles of palisades: past Herculaneum where from the shot towers once there dropped globules of lead for Jackson at New Orleans: past the mouth of the *Rivière à Saint Joachim* (which Americans call the *Swashin*), entering from hills inhabited by descendants of the Creoles who named it: past Saint Nicholas Rock and Cornice Rock— or nearly past. For some time back we have been steering to an island that sits in midstream, a tight bouquet of shade in the trembling heat. Over a beach of quartz that shimmers and burns we walk to a cottonwood grove. Here the leaves rattle like the pages of a book left in the open, and here the ground is moist and cool. We flatten our bellies to it, rub our backs in it. Before we drop asleep, we lie watching through branches the clouds enormous and still, packed with the fissures and convolutions of brains.

Wakened by voices toward evening we see two boys on the sand shelf below—one standing, holding a rusty tin can; the other digging. They are dark-skinned and black eyed, exquisitely easy in motion. To me they are familiar types. Sticking my head out over the bank, twisting my neck, twisting my grammar and pronunciation, I call down:

*"Quoi c'est qu' t'es après gratter là, mon p'tsit?"*

The boy who is digging starts, letting three turtle eggs fall from his brown hand. Instead of answering my question he exclaims:

*"Mais tu charres le français?"*

*"Faut crouère!"*

*"Mais t'es pas d'icitte? Tu charres pas tout comme n's aut'?"*

*"Possible. J'sieu pas d'icitte, non. Et touè? Tu restes pas tout de même d'dans l'île?"*

*"Non: à Crystal City. Là-bas à l'aut' bord, là."*

And he points to the mainland. His father and a great many other Missouri hill Creoles (descendants of the original French settlers) are employed in the glass "works" of Crystal City.

From this camp, meaning to enjoy the day while it is good, we push off before sun in chill so crisp that we keep on our parkas—the while, however, our legs are bare, covered with gooseflesh below shorts that serve as breech-

clouts. On such mornings we are twitching with gaiety the
more forceful because we attempt to repress it. When
the pilot, starting to the boat with the motor, treads too
near the edge of a sand shelf; when, without warning,
both pilot and motor are moulded in the beach below, the
other two of us drop our load and lie in the sand also,
helpless with mirth. But we make no sound. The curses
of the pilot are whispered. Our laughter is muffled. We
are like wild cubs that even in play must cushion a fall,
making no report. We shove from the shore without a
word. Why? Because the slightest sound rolls as in a
well-mouth; because the river pours milk and silver from
a mist; because in the gray cold, with dew bellied flat
on a leaf or hanging, pyriform, from twigs, the whole
wretched globe is fresh as the inner pink of shells. Man
is happy. His weight is light on the fan-shaped bones of
his foot; the flex of his torso delights; in his hollow wind-
pipe breath is sweet. Such glee inclines to silence, not to
talk. There is already in it a foretaste of regret. One
watches it hard while it is there to be watched, as one stares
at the balls of light that move out in a sheaf from rockets.

Once in midstream we are lost in alternate patches of
weak sun and mist. There are glimpses of cliffs superbly
tall. Fog streams off them inshore, so that their bulk
seems to float outward toward us. Then for a while, as
the Illinois shore has already been flat, the Missouri shore
becomes so. On the left, far in from the water, bluffs wall
off the prairies. Others on the right, far inland, bound
the hills and the wheat of southern Missouri. Between

these two lines of cliffs distance is measured in terms of
plains. Islands stand low along shore and bars jut out, all
flat. Their oaks and elms, to be seen at all from where we
are, must be gigantic; yet they resemble the architect's
toys in his model to scale. The scene is vast. And what
we are seeing, across its breadth, is the departure of night
from a side of the globe. It strangles my gaiety as sometimes music, meaningless at first, works under my guard
without any warning, so that I must strive not to snivel
in public. As the notes move to their place in the com-
poser's design they give off a light. They illuminate certain sections, normally invisible, in the sector of time
called past. *William's dead, honey. William's gone. The
boys are coming to take Will, honey. Let me lift you up.*
Do I know or do I imagine that it was like this? Did I
lean from her arms, touching the plush of the coffin with
one finger, as if it were sticky? Did my other hand clutch
with the cloth of her dress the nipple where William had
fed? Why should I recall what I have never before remembered? What has it got to do with music? Have I
not gone quite astray from the music? But music is like
that. And now distance and wind and water in miles of
restless breast are like that, and night moving from North
America.

We try to find—unsuccessfully because it is blocked off
by islands—the mouth of the pretty little *Rivière à l'Eta-
blissement.* Nor can we see, on the left, the restoration of
the *Fort de Chartres,* the old stronghold, nerve-knot of
French authority between Quebec and New Orleans. We

tie up instead at Little Rock where there is no settlement but a landing for the town of Sainte Genevieve.

Waiting for the boys to arrange for a visit ashore, I saunter over to a tug (*Port of Memphis*) and go on board where two men, obviously brothers, wave me to a seat without stopping their talk. They are indignant because. on the Little Rock Road last night, they saw a county sheriff stop his car to reprimand a fellow who was walking with his arm around a woman.

"They sho by God got funny ways up heah."

"If *Ah'd* a-ben walking with a young lady lak that an' he'd ha' said what he said t'me, then he jest hadn't ought to ha' done it!"

I sit looking at them, at the length of their bodies, the breadth of their shoulders, the unclouded berry-blue candor of their eyes; remarking the paradox of their easy good nature and their fractious independence. It occurs to me that I am in the presence of two Confederate sol- diers. The dates would not jibe. The men are young. But in essence I am right. They are the latest in a chain of corporeal continuity. They are Southern frontiersmen, so literally my people that in trouble I should have to go with them though I knew myself marked to drop in the first fire.

One of the brothers tells me of his life. He was born on the Cumberland near Nashville. From the first he lived on water and had some kind of little *bateau*. (He pro- nounces it *bat-teau*.) In that region he has his old lady and kids. Sometimes he tries farming just to be with them. But he can't stand it long. "Seem lak Ah git th' all-ovahs if Ah'm off wheah Ah kain' heah no ole boats a-hootin'." He speaks of the camaraderie of the boatmen; how they sleep and board one another free, and go without charge to one another's aid. "A man that's lived on the rivah an' knows the rivah ain' going t'have t'be told what the rivah kin do." He has chilly respect for the work of the government engineer. "Ah wish Ah had me a little of the money theah th'owing away. Lissen t'me, man: the ole rivah's goin' to behave jest as long as the ole rivah wants to behave. Then the ole rivah's a-goin' wheah the ole rivah wants to go." And this is of course the opinion of many an observer from De Soto down to our day.

My friends return, their arrangements complete. The *Ni-sho-dse* is to remain with the captain of the ferryboat, the *F. X. Roth.* And we are going to stay a few days in Grandmother's house, behind the big ginkgo tree. There, in the tall rooms nobody will say: "Boys, get your feet off the chairs." It will be: "Boys, what would you like to eat? Melissa has a chicken and a *brindgème** and some gumbo, and some corn and tomatoes and a cake. She's freezing some cream. What shall we add?" And better than her thought for boys' greed will be the love in her voice; the mild unshattered and unshatterable courtesy of her bearing.

*Creole French for *aubergine*, eggplant.

119

# Where the Rivers Meet

In Sainte Genevieve we are so well known that even the old negress Delphine, the washerwoman, gives us welcome home. She is visibly as French as African, nor does the complication of her line end there. *"Ma mère,"* she says, *"c'était eunne sauvagesse, eunne Quiquapoux."* In her deep voice (and in English which, like her French, is of good colloquial stuff) she asks my youngest companion if he remembers the day when he came with François on the pony to her cabin, when they were thrown off in the *Rivière à Gaboury,* and when she stood them naked as from the womb behind the stove while she dried their clothes? "Ah," she adds, examining the young man as if she had not seen him before, "time passes; boys grow."

We leave her, to walk about the village. No man who has known it can return without bright eyes and a quick step. If the government of Missouri were on its toes it would throw up fortifications about the place, posting troops to keep out tourists.

Sainte Genevieve had its beginnings back around 1723, when miners (under grant from the *Fort de Chartres*) began to get out lead from the interior. It has suffered change of course, yet the postern gate of an old convent is still here, the Villon-Papin house; the Guibourd house; the Bolduc (or Bois-le-duc) house; the Saint Gemme de Beauvais and the Amoureux house, with stables, slave quarters, gardens. In spirit and flavor it is miraculously whole. It was put here by men who fought river and wilderness not to make a camp, but a little French town. They lie now under the green of the cemetery: *Ci-git* (and

*Ici repose*) Govereau, Boverie, Leclerc, La Rose, Tho-
mure, Vallée, Rozier. Such was their character, such the
receptive land, that their imprint went deep and stayed.
Not the influx of Americans, not the invasion of Germans
with incredible names—nothing has yet effaced its charm.

In the evening we go looking for the priest, an old
friend who stutters in two languages with excitement to
see us; who pulls us through the door of the presbytery,
not knowing which to embrace first. *"Ah,"* he says to me
when we are settled, *"on se fait vieux. C'est donc toi qui
descendras à la cave. Tu vas trouver, à gauche en entrant,
un petit porto exquis."* He gives me a candle and, among
the webs in the dank grime, I lay hand to a bottle with
the good date.

Behind the columns of an arcade we sit sipping; between
us and a moonlit shoulder of the apse, a garden with
mockingbirds hard at their song. Ah, the good South! *Ah,
cette bonne, cette chère vallée du Mississippi!*

Below Sainte Genevieve we enter the mouth of the Kaskaskia. It is much smaller than the Illinois but, like it,
plump and full and quiet. It also, in colonial days, made
a good road. After half an hour of green willows, green
water and air, of plopping fish and turtles sliding from
logs, we turn back to the Mississippi, sleepy as if we had
been staring into the flame of a hearth. Before long we
are at the site of the village of Old Kaskaskia.

In the last years of the seventeenth century, driven by
the Iroquois from their home on the Illinois, the Kaskaskia

Indians came here. And with them came Jesuits and traders and gathering settlers. They made a French town that grew in size and influence until, before Sainte Genevieve, before Saint Louis, it was a Mother of the West. Here, after the partial destruction and abandonment of the *Fort de Chartres,* the English came to build Fort Gage. And here in turn, in 1778, George Rogers Clark ran up the flag of the young republic. Whether he did or not emerge from the shadows about a door to say that the dance might go on, but in Virginia's name not England's, he certainly lay with his few men along the river bank till dark, barked at by the dogs, alone in a big territory with a big idea.

This village, which men might piously have preserved, has been wholly destroyed. The Mississippi in one of its rampages cut overland some six miles above the mouth of the Kaskaskia, appropriating to itself the bed of the smaller stream, widening it, eating away the land of the settlement, giving the citizens barely time to pull on their pants. Today one house is left on the slope of the hills that rose behind the old town. It was the home of a local great man, Pierre Ménard, and is worthy yet to house a person of distinction. It is a gracious, deep-galleried place with sloping roof and mansard windows, having in all dimensions that extra half-yard that makes for spaciousness, that one more ounce in the balance of simplicity which makes for taste. It is a type of which there are yet others across in Missouri, and a great many on the plantations of Louisiana.

# The Mississippi

On the hill behind it are the earthworks of Fort Gage, grown now with a wood. From its shade one looks far out over the country—over the Mississippi rounding a flat point of the mainland opposite, receiving a little tributary as on a relief map; and over Kaskaskia Island (left between the old channel and the new).

Descending, we cross to the island and, afoot over its desperate flatness, we set out for a hamlet called New Kaskaskia. There, in a commonplace little church, is a bell saved from the flood. It is dated 1747 and inscribed *Pour L'église des Illinois*. In an outbuilding behind a cottage near by we are shown a stone bearing a cross and the date 1737. It lies under a grindstone, by a heap of shucked corn. Scared pullets run between our legs as we stoop to examine it.

The stone has been considered by the family of the place as a sort of good-luck piece, carried by them in their several removes. By the present owner it is kept with special regard because of visitors' interest and their offers of money. Those who beg him never to dispose of it without consulting them are told: "Ye ain't t'fret!" He remembers the destruction of Kaskaskia. The rivers were high one afternoon, and from the bank he wuz a-tossin sticks fer his ole dawg to retrieve when he noticed the water a-runnin in and a-runnin out—you fellers knows the way high water'll do: then the bank begun to give and before night damn him if it wuzn't devil git the hindmost.

His vexation is comic when his memory fails. He feels cheated that in youth he did not know he would be a

123

landmark later. He would have picked other things to keep and remember:

"Why, godamit, me 'n' Baptis' LaRose has fed horses an' drank whiskey many's the time under Ménard's gallery. How the hell'd I know they's a-goin t'polish them floors and bring in all them folks a-wantin' me t'tell'm this an' that?"

After a silence, scrutinizing the horizon, he adds: "I still drink whiskey when I kin git it."

Reaching the boat late in the afternoon, footsore and hot, we turn gratefully to midstream, sending the *Nisho-dse* so hard through the quickening water that her prow gives off a slobber. Beyond Chester we turn into an island, a tangled willow thicket with beaches at the lower end facing Missouri, mounting backwards in tablets of sand toward Illinois. Along all the shore there are parallel tracks of turtles, interrupted by claw marks where they have stood on their hind legs to mount the shelves. Many of these trails we follow to their end, hoping to find eggs; but where every turtle stopped, a boy has left the print of his foot and knee.

The sun goes down in a colored dust of light, opal and silver, then lusterless slate starred by fireflies. The rim of the island is indented, having wet fingers of sand that stand like the grain of a board. Between these the water enters and runs out with the look and sound of a falling tide. Soon the beach is white and to sleep we must turn our backs upon the candid moon.

# The Mississippi

Waking, breakfasting on a shore kept alive with wake of passing boats, we set out for one more morning of limitless distance, of heat and light that seem to suck me up a pipe, dispersing me until consciousness is a mild catalyst permitting—but barely—a register of sensation. Toward noon we reach the mouth of the Saint Côme. Its water, backed up by that of the Mississippi, scarcely moves. It has a blackish green medicinal look, carpeted so evenly with cotton from the willows that the *Ni-sho-dse,* like an ice-breaker, leaves a path. Since the water is clear, we can see far down and know we are convoyed by numbers of gars with pig eyes and grotesque swords. We follow back to the bluffs which form the Cape Saint Côme, so called because the Jesuit Jean François Buisson de Saint Côme is said to have ascended them (in December, 1698). The river is correctly named in full the *Rivière du Cap Saint Côme,* but no French place name of the region has had more comic misadventure. First of all, at the hands of its own kin: the Creoles themselves have confused *Saint Côme* with *Cinq Hommes.* And the Americans after them have made it Cape St. Combs, St. Cormes, Sink Home, Singe Homme, and even *Capes-and-Combs!*

By evening, idling beneath the good range of bluffs of the Missouri shore, we have come upon an object which has been for centuries a curiosity. The Mississippi, for a short distance relatively narrower, swings into a bend where, coming in from the right, there enters the little *Rivière à Brazeau.* Below it the current, making from the more to the less restricted channel, dashes at a high rock,

125

isolated from the Missouri bank. The rock is called by the French *La Grande Tour* and by the English Grand Tower. Marquette speaks of the "violent struggle" and "great din" caused by separation of waters about it, inspiring "terror in the savages, who fear everything." Indians who accompany Saint Côme in 1698 report that fourteen Miamis have been lost there and that all passing are accustomed to offer sacrifice. Thereupon the Jesuit, to prove that his medicine is biggest, ascends the rock, plants a cross singing the *Vexilla Regis,* and fires three volleys of musketry.

Innocent of any danger, we approach the rock and allow ourselves to be drawn around it into the half circle of channel that shuts it from the mainland. But not once, until we have emerged at the far end, do we remember to examine the rock. We are pulled as if by the hair into a current hard and triumphant, broken by whirlpools that smack like alligators turning in a tank. There is one especially, impressive not so much for its size (there is no room for the big ones we meet in midstream) as for the deep humming cone at its center. We get over safely because of our momentum—and because we draw little water —but we are jostled abruptly as when, in a wheeled vehicle, one hits a bump. We are told later by local residents that we have been very foolish; that whole trees, floating into that channel, come out "all ground up."

For the moment we know only that the weather, cheaply melodramatic, is attempting to surround our danger with dark and with crash of thunder. Below the great rock, on the only soil visible among the stones of the bank, we pitch the tent; surround it with a ditch; and settle for a long summer evening. There is rain on the roof and the mill-wheel churn of a steamer laboring upstream. Through the flaps of the door we see a section of river, its surface covered with bouncing drops as with the leaping of millions of fleas.

This morning I am able to inspect the Tower. At the present stage it emerges from the water to a height of perhaps seventy-five feet on the shore side. Its oval bulk lurches forward toward midriver. Floods have nibbled it at so many levels that it seems to be composed of thin tablets of lime, grooved with perpendicular cracks where its weight has shifted. On its top there must be a fair depth of soil; there is grass and a growth of young trees. Such a pile, gray, pitted, and sprouted with fern, seen over the dull mirror of water; with the moan of doves indistinguishable from the echo of the moan of doves against the crags—all this has inspired many a pretty passage in the diaries of steamboat days.

We push off in a sullen, sultry morning, with shadows that quickly appear and quickly fade until the sun comes out for good, steaming up the moisture of last night's rain. Addled with heat and brightness we take refuge in the shady mouth of Apple Creek (the French *Rivière à la Pomme*). The steamer *Peniman*, passing downstream, shoves such a force of wake against us that we push farther inland and then, discovering that we are in a charming

wood-heart, farther still. Pulling under a tree, stopping
to free our propeller of weeds, we find under the same low
boughs an overalled man in a johnboat. He is a shanty-boat
fisherman, not at all unfriendly, not even shy, but drowsy,
and unwilling to spend energy in greetings. As we nose
in beside him he points down without a word to the black
water where two gars, one at least five and a half feet
long, hang motionless an instant and then sink down. He
observes dispassionately: "Them sons of bitches." Then
he yawns.

But he wakes abruptly at the mention of Indians. The
Shawanese and Delawares, brought here as a bulwark
against the Osages and the Americans in 1793, were given
land between this stream and the Saint Côme by the Baron
de Carondolet. "Is that a fact?" inquires our friend, looking at me as if at last I am talking sense. He is aware that
this ground has been well populated by savages, because
of the "relics" he picks up. His imagination has been
fired. He has tried to picture the country as it was then.
Half ashamed of his enthusiasm he stops speaking, sitting
humped over his reflection. Then, with light in his eye,
he looks up quickly to add: "Man, they tell me game was
plenty then!"

He has heard it from the sons of the sons. They tell him;
he has not read it. Something stings me to attention also;
something in his voice, its wonder, its hypnotic unrest, its
nostalgia for a place known not to the man but to his blood
before him. Here before me is the type that moved out
ahead of the successive frontiers to the Pacific: the fellow

128

always ready to pick up and go, who disappeared to return for Marthy and the chaps when he had made a little crop somewhere off beyond where things were going to be better; where he could breathe and fetch a holler when he felt full of vinegar in the frost of morning; where he could run a few traps and make a little salt and nowhere be repressed.

And the man adds, still to his reflection: "Man, I'd go tomorrer."

Dodging the wake of a Paducah steamer, we push out downstream around a series of bends in which Missouri stands fortified against the East with cliffs whose scars glow in the evening light. As we move toward those called Hanging Dog and the Devil's Tea Table, there falls an exquisite hush over the river. Sheltered from view by the bluffs, we do not see the sky where it gathers storm. Ignorant, we accept the abrupt cool, the stillness that carries to the rock our lowest word. Soon it is too late to choose a camp. Unless we are willing to ride out a bad half-hour we must land at once. Turning ashore, we find a broad rock floor, base of an old cliff, no doubt, at the water's edge. Here, since there is no soil, we weight the corners of the tent with rocks. Then, having made what preparation we can, we stand bare-legged in the foam to watch. Actually we are not harmed, or even rained upon. We are once more so placed that we may watch, exempt the while, the weather of the world. To the left the view is walled by bluffs wooded and scarred; to the right it is bounded by Illinois, flat, and with every willow leaning east in wind.

Between the two is the river, immense and leaping. Over the sunset moves a storm, the one untold miles from the other, but for us mingling in one thing. And what we see in the sky we see in the water, vastness for vastness. The sky, from light blue turns dark, bruised. Instantly the width of the Mississippi likewise is bruised, the teeth of its white caps sickly slate. For a moment the storm fails. There is a gap in its force. The sky, a moment orchid, floods with a wild salmon—the river recording both changes, pitching in its whole bulk violet, then orange. After a moment, bellied and full, the storm breaks. Rain, like a column of dust, stands high and moves thinning out in wind. It spreads over the sunset, ribbing it with fine lines, filming it with a lavender webby haze. Among the willows of Illinois it touches the surface of the globe and crashes, brisk, with the crackle of a well-fed flame. Above it sit packed high banks of cumulus clouds, shot with hot threads of lightning, flushed from within so that their shape is briefly plain. And their flanks are white as snow is white under the moon.

Then there is utter quiet. The sky is clear, with flat herringbone clouds too high and feebly violet to register in water. The moon comes up, lighting the river and our rock as if they were one. When a brilliantly lighted steamer passes, sending crest after bubbling crest to flatten out over the stone almost at my head, I seem afloat with no bed and no home, no continent, no world. It is a little as if I waked to find myself over an abyss, crossing on a narrow springy plank; yet for so quickening a sense of night and space I am willing to pay with my night's sleep.

This morning I go inland for water along a path barely traced in blooming red clover. I have the path to myself except for a half-grown rabbit that sits nibbling wind, trembling until I come close. He dives away, a spot of white flag and brown hind feet flat below the hock.

A country doctor, owner of the first farm I find, accompanies me to the cistern. While our reflection is troubled by drops from the bucket, while my hands draw in the cold hair of the rope, he tells me that where we are camped is Moccasin Spring—but that the spring itself is twenty odd feet, for the moment, under the flooded Mississippi. Here in the late autumn of 1838 the Cherokees, in their "Trail of Tears," ferried the river. Fourteen thousand of them, banished from their home in the southern mountains, came up this bank, turning through these hills to Arkansas and Oklahoma, without hope, homesick and slow. The doctor, at a political rally far inland (and thirty years ago), mentioning that he owned land at Moccasin Spring, was drawn aside by an old Indian who remembered the crossing. His brother had died in the camp of that night. He thought he might, if one would permit him to go back, even find the grave.

From such a spot we leave reluctantly and late. A few miles beyond, preceded by herons that move in long fluctuating lines from island to island as we approach, we

enter the big bend around the Cap à Girardeau (or Girardot). Girardot, an ensign with the royal troops at
Kaskaskia in 1704, is known to have resigned his com-
mission to engage in the Indian trade. It is supposed that
he came here for his barter, and that his name was given
to the cape by early boatmen. Here the Mississippi
does all a river can do with tremendous breadth and graceful scatter of islands. From so small a craft as ours (except
for the dovetailing currents, for the weight and lunge
of the water in one direction) there is not necessarily the
impression that we are on a river at all.

Yet the town of Cape Girardeau, as we draw near it, has
nothing of the lake or seacoast. A trading post was built
on this site in 1793 by Lorimier, the French counterpart
of Simon Kenton and Sevier. In his life, marriage with a
squaw, capture of Boone, removal of the Shawanese to the
west bank of the river, were three meager details. The
town which grew up about his post, slowly and naturally,
with no boom of gold or oil, has come up from and become
a part of the river bank. It is a great wonder that moving-
picture producers have not spotted its waterfront. By removing billboards, by roping off its street from motor-
driven vehicles, it could be made the scene of any portrayal
of steamboat life in the '60's. The levee, paved with humped
cobblestones, slopes down from a good height to the river.
It is flanked by brick warehouses with tall arched windows,
their long row broken into by the entrance of a street at
the end of which, topping terrace after green terrace,
rises the courthouse. The city which has grown about it is

brisk and clean, with little of the urban area's dismal blight. Before it is the Mississippi; behind it rolling field and wood.

Below Cape Girardeau the river is divided by an island for a long way; its water on the surface calm, but knotty underneath, jolting and nervous. It regains its mile of width at the end of the island, moving unobstructed to Thebes, in Illinois. Here we put in briefly, attracted by the look of the lower town, oldish and pleasantly crumbly, with stairs mounting to the upper town. Having noted on the height a building with balcony and colonnade, stoutly made of stone covered with plaster which has partly chipped off, I enter a bar to ask what it may be. The bartender stops, hand outstretched to the wet towel, and, with mouth open, considers me an instant: "Why hell, man, that's the old courthouse!"

That is the kind of answer I always get, in a tone of wonder, impatience, or disgust. I am everywhere like the transcontinental aviator who, landing in a fog, calling out to know his location, is told that he is in Charlie Driscoll's cow-pasture. But I am secretly pleased by the implication of such replies. It flatters an atavistic desire to be born, to have one's son and to die in the same house; to have one home on a knoll from which to survey the rest of the world. Absorbed in this, I have no great interest when the bartender adds: "Lincoln and Douglas debated up there."

There being nowhere to camp by the town, we push off in gathering dusk, coming to shore lower down on the Missouri side above the village of Commerce.

## Where the Rivers Meet

The tent sits on the sloping sand, surrounded by willows which grow down even into the water, shaking and trembling where it moves into a "riffle." Tonight we have the white moon again and may move about as by day, not groping or falling. We even set out for a walk, discovering that the tangled hill behind us is grooved by a road along its flank. In heavy grass two parallel ruts lead out, filled with dust soft as if it had been scraped from the wings of moths. They follow the river, barely holding off to either side an exuberant growth of sassafras, trumpet vine, sumac and honeysuckle. The smell gives a milky heaviness to the air. All this, protected by the hill, huddled where it is frequently beaded by river mist, is exceptionally lush. The sycamore leaf I pluck in walking by is twice in width the span of my fingers; and blackberries, gleaming from the drooping briars, are as long as a joint of my thumb.

We pad on in the white dust, with now on the left a wide expanse of moonlit river through the trees, and now on the right from a dark "draw" a column of cold air. In a bend (dumbfounded to find such a thing in such a place), we come upon a deserted brick and terra cotta plant, and beyond it the shacks of the folk who were employed in it. There is a tangle of old cars, junk, weedy garden and shanty architecture. They are lustily hemmed, invaded already by vegetation that will not wait for complete decay. There has evidently been sorrow and privation here, and we are decently grieved. But, with the fact accomplished, we may admit that it is heartening to see the healthy earth slough off the scar; to have evidence that, however the sorry race may fail, the incoercible leaven underneath yields nowhere except for the moment.

Climbing a hill we come upon the first house of the village of Commerce. It, too, is abandoned; a "mansion" of the '80's or '90's, in cracker-box style. A boy who falls into step with us here tells that after a death in the family, after a funeral held on the porch, not a soul re-entered the house. "They wuz heart-broke." Leaving the interior just as it happened to be, they "all went back to Mississippi." If the story is untrue it will prosper nonetheless, so does the locale become a dismal legend.

In the village proper we enter a shack that serves as pool-room and beer saloon combined. Yesterday's *Globe* is on the bar, heavily thumbed at the column giving stages of the river. Behind the bottles, against the dim mirror, leans an advertisement showing a girl in navy jacket and pants that mold her body. She seems inflated by air. A wag has drawn an arrow to the point where he would like to see a puncture occur. Old men and boys are bent over cards under a fly-specked droplight in the corner. They are seated on orange crates and metal ice-cream parlor chairs that have the backs sawed off. In the center of the room balls click over a table to which a little felt still sticks. One player has an anchor in the hair of his forearm, blue and red. The other wears a belt set with glittering stones. On the swivel seats of the bar we talk with a barge man. He is wide eyed, decent and friendly. He tells of a cemetery on the hill that dominates the town; of the headstones with dates that go back to the eighteenth century. A man can see bones in the gullies after a hard rain. And who were those people? "They's steamboat men and some of thesyur o-o-old farmers."

Across the street on a vacant lot there lies a boat half-built. The owner "took and lit out for Colorado." Most of the town has lit out for somewhere it seems, leaving home to the alder and sumac. Yet the village square they have left is sweet beneath the moon: the frame building, small in its large plot, marked with the wavering sign *City Hall;* the grass-grown sidewalk with the fallen branch that no one moves aside; the boy with his arm around a girl on the old church steps. The girl is teasing a kitten with a switch. It rolls on its back gathering all four paws to its navel in mirth. Then it walks away sedately. Picking it up I see that its eyes, even by moonlight, are blue, and that its little tab of a tongue is pink.

Returning to camp, capping the hill by the dark "mansion," we overtake two tiny boys returning with a tinier sister to their home among the shanties. When I ask what could have brought them out so late, one of them replies: "We-uns had two pinnies [pennies]." They ask if we mind walking slowly so that they may keep up: they are frightened after dark. "Men gits t'playin' poker in them empty houses. Then they gits mad an' runs out a-hollering an' a-shootin'." The road is of sharp gravel. Since it is difficult to keep in motion at all and not leave behind little sister, I pick her up and would carry her. Instantly she pushes from my shoulders with both hands, shrieks, and drums with her feet against my stomach. I am obliged to put the little creature down, to let it begin, unshod among the stones, its destiny as a woman by the river.

In camp, silence and the hum of water over rock. Above and behind the tent, a dry clicking from the Tom Good Light (miles 40.4 above Cairo: Fl. W. 2 sec.). Somewhere in the State of Illinois a hound dog bays. From downstream comes the pant of a steamer. At the bend she appears, shoving before her a load of oil barges with a raucous *Oh*-ha! *Oh*-ha! The superstructure, except for running lights, is dim; the lower deck is bright. She is smoky and powerful—with the kitten and little sister, part of the same night.

We are wakened this morning by the tearing of breakers, and lay hold of the glasses in time to read *Illinois* on the side of a boat disappearing downstream with barges in the sun and mist. In sight, coming downstream also, rapidly, with no load, is the *H. L. Duffey*, her tow-knees crumbling foam. Her wake, added to that of the *Illinois*, makes a fine disturbance on the shore.

This is Sunday, and hot so soon after sunrise. We vote not to move. Among boulders that have broken and rolled from the hill we breakfast and loll under the willows. They have grown like cane or bamboo. Over us cuckoos with their white throat and checkered tail crane and twist to watch. When we have lain still for a while a whole world of song sparrows, vireos and warblers come down close about our shoulders so that their shadows mingle with the flicker of the shadows of leaves, and we have, beside their song, the casual, meditative notes they sound when at ease amongst themselves.

At fifteen minutes after nine the *Golden Eagle* passes on her way to Alabama. We have ridden her and know her staunch captain. She is the last vessel of a line (passed from father to son to grandson) that for seventy-five years has provided such sights as this we see—a white boat trailing wake. Troops have crowded the rails: guns have sent balls whistling over the bows: trains and trucks have eaten into profits: but the vessels and the men of the line, faithful to something greater than governments and dollars, have kept to the river.

The shore, from the passing of the *Golden Eagle*, shakes and trembles for a quarter of an hour with incoming water. Then comes the *Iowa* with six barges, the *Jane Rhea* and an unidentified boat from New Orleans. All morning the little breakers move into the willows, separating at their trunks, uniting behind them, hissing and stopping in a flounce of foam.

At evening there comes the packet *Washington,* larger than the *Golden Eagle* and as white, from a port in Ohio —which, we cannot make out. She appears in the bend below out of a bank of mist, just under the disc of the moon. She catches and scatters in her wake its light, invisible yet where the water is smooth. Elegant, her pilot house like a howdah, she steams off graceful and grand, leaving us like little boys, chagrined that we are not connected with so much glory.

# The Mississippi

I spend the first half of the night (until the mosquitoes become too bad) balanced in the canoe among the quaking shrubs. The moonlight falls on the yellow shellac of the ribbing around me. When after midnight I am driven in, the shelf of beach I see from the tent is so bright that between half-closed eyes it is not distinguishable from water. Our door seems fitted to the river's edge.

At sun-up a tolling and thudding of waves. Either a very large boat has just passed, or one of any size has come very close. The *Ni-sho-dse* is full of water; the stern line is snapped, the head line loose. The shore is wet and winking with a new boundary of spray.

Since we have left Cape Girardeau the appearance of the river has begun to change. There have been no bluffs; the hills are fewer and more grudgingly spaced. Below Commerce the change is complete. Moving toward its meeting with the Ohio, the Mississippi takes on a look unequalled except in the wild hundred miles to the sea, below New Orleans in the delta. Here in this stretch it rounds a peninsula of Illinois jutting into Missouri, flowing for a time north and a little east. Then it doubles a finger of Missouri jutting into Illinois, making thereafter straight southeast to Cairo. In all of this no road is visible. On neither peninsula does the map show any settlement. Illinois is flat and green. Missouri is flat and green: it moves off into an area once labelled *Great Swamp*. Popularly it is still called Swampeast Missouri. The term is no longer just, but there was a time when it was earned. In days when the most commonplace of the valley would have been wild to us, this region was thought especially wild. In the mid-eighteenth century the city of New Orleans dispatched expeditions here to kill and salt down a winter supply of buffalo and elk. One century later, when the frontier had crept round and gone West, there were still buffalo and elk. They lived in the deep-grass islands, protected by a maze of bayous, by stagnant crescent lakes and pools of black seep water. The Creoles of upper Louisiana knew the region as a hunting ground for bear and beaver. They went down the Saint François, the Black, the Castor, the Whitewater. They brought out furs and tubs of bear fat. They floated them on to the Arkansas or poled them up to Cape Girardeau. A century later there were still bear.

Then came the earthquake of 1811. Men who had known their way among the bayous had to start again from scratch. Water was driven upstream. Channels were changed; new lakes impounded. Strange divides arose. The drainage system was re-formed.

It was slow hard work when settlements began to appear inland on the ridges. Folks came down with the "agger," with fever, with the "weak jerks" and the "bloody flux." They were bony and green in the face. They "waggoned" in supplies with solid wooden wheels. They got out to throw logs across the mud holes. They rode on mile-long timber bridges where the gumbo was too deep. They got over to one side when cattlemen came by a-horseback, floundering joyously in the round-up. Men and mounts were splattered. Their eyeballs and their teeth were very white.

In our time the government has decreed drainage ditches every quarter of a mile. That assures a stable ground. It opens soil that is bottomless and rich beyond the dream of Egypt. Yet even this discipline has not robbed the place of its wild tang. Its swans and parakeets are no more. But pelicans come up from the South. In autumn there is the snake bird big as a goose, fending the dark water with his neck as he swims half submerged. Moccasins hold up their finger heads among the cypress knees. The sky is black with ducks at times. And there are game fish moving over the black silt floor of pools, threading bubbles of the seepage.

The Mississippi loses none of its strength as it flows through here. But it reflects and concentrates the mood of the land. It is full and quiet. It has an odor of rotting, not unpleasant, like the smell of an unfamiliar tea. Mile after mile there is nothing to look at but bare sand islands. They are lemon colored against the engulfing green. Their shore and the herons and killdeer that walk their shore are all distorted by the flicker of heat. The mainland to either side is a jungle. Whether its trees are great or small we do not know. We have lost all clue to scale. We stare at the miles of river; at the willow wall that rises like the outer bristles of a brush. Out there the awkward heron lays her eggs, and muskrats zigzag under water sleek as moles. But if farms exist they are out of sight. Once in a while we see a shanty. It is propped on stilts. Its inmates

stare and wave as if they were marooned. And once we
come upon a squatter in a bay. His johnboat is moored
by a lean-to of willows. He gets up from a cot and flails
his arms about as we sweep on. Then no more houses.
No more boats or men. We are alone in silence as great as
the stillness of an antique world of tree ferns, of birds that
showed descent from snakes.

The sameness lulls us. The damp heat makes us drowsy.
There is nothing to tell us it is coming. There is no way
to know that the Ohio is just around the bend. Suddenly
we are staring at a width of two rivers, the shores of three
states, Illinois, Missouri, Kentucky. The North and West
come down to meet the East in a deep and easy socket.
They make no fuss. They move upon the South in quiet
tons.

~~~~~~~~~~~~~~~~~~~~~~~~~~~

## V

# THE OHIO AND THE TENNESSEE

~~~~~~~~~~~~~~~~~~~~~~~~~~~

## V

# The Ohio and the Tennessee

IN DAYS BEFORE our race lived on the Ohio, the Ohio
had no inhabitants. We are the first whose foolhardi-
ness, or whose need, has driven us to live by its very
shores. In prehistoric times (as men may see by remains
of the mound builders), and in Indian times, the immediate banks of the Ohio were judged unfit for human
dwelling.

Seeing the river for what it was, finding that it "rolled
down a dark valley where the sun hardly shone long
enough to dry the masses of driftwood," the Indians
located their chief seats far inland on the tributaries:
Delawares on the Muskingum, Shawanese on the Scioto,
Wyandots and Ottawas on the Maumee, Weas, Kickapoos
and Pottawatomies on the Wabash.

These streams enter the Ohio all from the north. To
the south, in Kentucky and western Virginia, there were no
men. No tribe, in history or tradition, ever made its home
there—unless, briefly and long ago, there was an extension
along the Cumberland of the Shawanese settlements. The
region was left as a hunting ground, shared, though not

always peaceably, by all of the tribes to the north of the
Ohio; by the Iroquois from beyond the Allegheny, from
the Long House of the Six Nations; and by tribes whose
range lay south of the Cumberland Mountains.

The whites, when they penetrated here, met resistance
unusually stiff. In some way never fully explained to us
a kind of sanctity lay on this land, for the Indian, so that
he defended it with special fury. It was a home of gods
as well as deer. He called it the *Hollow Land* because of
the many caves. And because caves, according to the temperature of the season, inhale or exhale, he called it also
the *Breathing Land*. The fact that he could, physically,
feel the breath of the god, made for him an equivalent
of the wounds of Christ.

Here it is not difficult to share the savage's point of
view. A man of any racial heritage, at the mouth of a great
cave, is stirred. At its threshold he leaves the ordinary.
Even so common a thing as air is new, and there is stillness more aggressive than any sound. He has stepped into
a secrecy that utters nothing and makes no move, watching,
to see. There drops on him knowledge that he is not now
with kingdoms animal and vegetable, to which he is related and in which he has made his home. He is in a gate
of a mineral realm sinking to depths where he has no
place, a bottomlessness where gems are formed and coal
takes the print of fish. Looking out the mouth, hairy with
silhouette of fern and columbine, the light he sees is violent
and too clear. Familiar objects are oddly precise in it,
so that again and again he examines them as he looks

at sea anemone through aquarium walls. He feels that he has happened upon an unguarded gap in the perimeter of time. And that is the truth. Outside in the light are instruments to gauge the fall of lime water from the roof: behind, in the black gullet, there is not time to measure.

The white men, when first they established themselves in this new west, held to the savage's rule in choosing sites. Bottom lands of the immediate river shore were rich, but they were few, separated by bluffs and in danger of flood. The whites kept also well to the interior. Only when the Ohio stood out clearly as the great path for western migration and eastward shipment of produce (and when steam seemed to assure regularity of this traffic) did men build permanent towns on the bank.

Thus Cairo exists almost literally at the mouth of the Ohio, and when the *Ni-sho-dse* has turned from the Mississippi, settling to the upstream pull, we begin at once to pass the "suburbs" of a port—lines of houseboats, of gangling shacks on stilts. Before we have adjusted ourselves to the change we are pulling up to a sloping levee, capped by a sea wall, above which spreads (as at Saint Louis, as at Cape Girardeau) another wood-block print of a river town. There are the typical brick buildings and the sign: *Planters' Hotel*. Moving in between the *Patricia* and the *Jane Barrett*, we tie up in a fleet of "skifts" and johnboats. Toward us from all over the levee white boys and black boys dart like schools of fingerling fish. To meet them, and to face their town, needs effort. We have this instant come from the flowing together of great streams. We are in the frame of mind of folk who wait the night from bed, watching in the sky an act performed by chance in their life span.

It is inevitable that Cairo should have a flavor Cairo's own. There are moving pictures and chain shops; the classic American drug store thrives. But these are plants whose seed has been blown or dropped by birds out of their native range. They exist against a background which takes tone from the fact that the town is lodged precariously between enormous rivers, on a thumb of soil to which history gives value unknown in the land office. Before us, for red tribes that thumb was goal and starting point. Before us, prime ministers pointed: "It is here, Sire, the joining of the Mississippi and the Ohio, *autrement dit la Belle Rivière.*" And for an instant as he leaned, the King brushed the map with the curls of his wig. The soil of Cairo has made a point of reference for the world.

As in Asia Minor the foundation of one town is discovered over that of another, or others, there is a Cairo over the Cairo of the Indians and the King's men. It is dated *circa 1860,* visible plainly in the galleried store buildings, in the "Opera Block," in the levee which was a concentration point for the Federal navy, and in the hotel where sat the man Grant (before Donelson, before Fort Henry) whetting his knife for the heart of the Confederacy.

Yet on top of that Cairo is another, contemporary with us. That is the Cairo of modern river traffic. Here there are no moth-eaten Indian feathers or Kings' wigs—not even the dwindling charm of the *ante-bellum*. Everything is crisply of our day and, as businesses go in these times, flourishing. People stare to hear it, but one may cite them figures. In 1881, peak year of the old packet steamers, there were moved in the Mississippi Valley system approximately 28,000,000 tons. In 1937, for the same system, the figure stood at 75,000,000. For this business Cairo is necessarily elbow- and knee-joint. Its waterfront has the ferment of meeting places. A man who has been sitting on the curb, back to a telephone pole, rises to tell me that it is "the most *poisonous* place for its size in the United States. Hit gits the rakins and scrapins from all over. Boys is hyar from the upper river and the lower river an' from the Missouri an' from the Ohio an' I hain't a-fergettin' the Hennepins. A man that ain't too perticular kin git anything he wants right hyar on Ohio Street, whether hit's a fight er a frolic er to save his soul an' give hit to Jesus Christ."

He walks with me a while, passing people who, like bats and moths, seem to be waiting for dusk. The black men say: "Gimme a cigarette, cap'n?" The white men say: "Got 'ny makins on ye, buddy?" and they use every accent from that of Saint Paul and Pittsburgh to that of New Orleans. A few girls are about, but with no requests or suggestions at this hour of day, moving with the air of saleswomen rearranging stock before customers are admitted. Standing before a bedraggled Mission I have pointed out the "fancy houses" and the *Glad Hand Saloon*

149

with its sign (inside): *Fight Guaranteed Every Thirty Minutes*. Considering the humanity left as by a drop in the flood on its levee, Ohio Street does, as my guide suggests, strike an enviable balance in its satisfaction of appetites.

However, it is necessary to believe that there are degrees in the social station of river boatmen, or that, like great artists (the one need begetting the other), they veer from a cloud-bank of *idéal* to the saw-dust floor of vice, and back. I do not know river men when they blubber hymns in the Mission, or when, anxiously, they count the nine days, having been out with Sadie to spend their stake. What I do know of them is this, that they have statuesque brown bodies which they use, at work, vigorously and with grace, as birds use wings; that they have in their eyes the candor of babies and the young of beasts; that with all their animal strength (and as if because of it) they are courteous, gentlemanly as Biblical herdsmen might be. I am not with them ashore and do not wish to be with them there. They are not shore dwellers. They must be judged as sea-birds are judged, not on the guano bed but aloft in flight.

Before Cairo runs the Ohio, full, and as broad at this moment as the Mississippi. To it have contributed the Monongahela, the Muskingum, the Scioto, the Kanawha, the Kentucky, the Wabash, the Cumberland and the Tennessee. Between them, though the drainage area of the Missouri is larger, they furnish one fourth of all the water that reaches the Gulf.

150

## The Ohio and the Tennessee

We face no easy task then, when we take off upstream.
And we do not go far. At Mound City, Illinois (where,
also, in the War were Federal navy yards), we stop to
consider. While we wait a boat comes down from Louisville, rapidly, kicking about her as with a skirt, an active
hem of foam. It is near night. The far bank is chalky pastel
green. Between it and us the broad water has a mulberry
overcast. As we sit resting we pass the glass from hand to
hand, keeping it trained on the Kentucky shore. From the
mouth of the Ohio to this point there has been little sign
of life in Kentucky, and there will be little until we reach
Paducah. For eighty miles the bank is (from the boat)
a delicate impenetrable jungle alive with birds. In Illinois
there is frequently the cry of a farmer to his horse, the
shrilling of a factory whistle, the small talk of commerce.
Against this, mile after mile, Kentucky opposes the soft-
ness of willows, the hush of woods, a silence that, like the
gaze of an owl, amounts to an accusation. The shore is low
and subject to inundation, separating from the river a
chain of lakes and ponds. It has not many inhabitants, even
inland. Thrusting the willows aside, stepping into one of
its clearings, it is as if, in a deserted house, you had broken
a membrane of gray web, over an alcove where the elab-
orate passive quiet glows like a last coal in ash. This is of
course not the fashionable part of Kentucky, but for men
who fear that industry will pave the globe with concrete
it is not an insignificant part.

Lying now on the Illinois bank, sweeping the long shore
opposite, suddenly, as one sights the "panorama" in an

Easter egg, we find a break in the green—a beach rising tier on tier of sand back from the river. We set out for it, striking at an angle the suave wake of the Louisville boat, savoring before we arrive the rest we shall have on the warm white sand.

When camp is made we are free to squat and look about. On either hand are cottonwoods old and tall, their roots fifteen feet out of earth; those on the water side perpendicular, those on the land side spread like the frame of a bustle. Behind us Kentucky is still, and so unused are men to the boon of soundlessness that we nearly find discomfort in it. It is as if we were being watched; as if something, possibly deer, were peering and seeing, turning from side to side, curious but trembling until we leave. It is not as when, on an island, we know the land to be circumscribed. Here there is an endlessness useless to explore. When we turn from woods it is to face an ardor of sunset—the Ohio under cold violet a hot orange; the active, still molten heart of a clear stone. We find little to say, and speak in the undertone men use when they lift their chin, squinting, to listen. There is wind and the moon rises, sending over the sand a dull glow; only, in the cottony froth of the water line there is on the foam a glistening, as in the trail of snails. What we might wish to say is too big and too slow for speech. And there are other ways to convey it. On the eyeball meaning can be read, as reefs or depths show on the top of water.

This morning there is no thought of leaving. The day

152

is moody, crumbling thunder back in Kentucky. Fitfully the scene clears, with submarine green-gold light, capped by the rainbow. The shore line before us is pounded by the cumbersome turf. It flags in and out, turning at a given distance as bears reverse direction, having paced a given length of cage. It moves upshore in a wall, poises and falls, striking first the upper point of the bay, unfurling, sidling along the beach. As it goes out it streams over sand, thinning to a film so shallow that it is wrinkled by the quartz grains under it. Immediately after it follows the band of wet, disappearing as the moisture is absorbed, so that the sand turns in color as paper browns before it burns. Between the thunder of Kentucky and that of the shore I sit out the morning under the willows, feet to the heckling foam, looking over at the great cow-bag of Illinois hanging south. I give the whole morning to it. It requires the whole morning to empty myself of the shoddy, the clever, the factual, the informative, the excelsior wadding of systems—thereby to make of myself an envelope to receive joy at the sight of this naked water having life. Afterwards, spiritually washed and replete, refuelled with courage, to the question "What's your b'iness?" or "What line y'in?" I should not hesitate to answer: "I stare at surf." They cannot jail me for it. Nor can they shake my conviction that true escapists go to football games, to night clubs and political rallies. Made to sit on a log in woods, with only doves moaning *Who? Oh, who? who?* they would see that, far from having escaped, they have moved out to the position which of all positions is most exposed.

After a second night on the echoing sand and a second morning of white caps, we conclude that this may be a constant condition on the Ohio. And we set out. Once off from the bank we are surrounded by excited teats of water, shoving up to the wind that beheads them whitely. This the *Ni-sho-dse* seems to enjoy. She raises and thrusts down her prow into foam as a work-horse unharnessed slobbers and sucks at the trough.

For a while there are few signs of life, even in Illinois. From the map it would appear that the village of Olmsted is not far. To make sure of this we pull up beside a moored shanty boat and call out:

"Hey! Are we far from Olmsted?"

"Don't reckon ye air."

We are startled as if caught in fault, because the voice does not come from the boat whence we expected it, but from the bank above. There, like the figurines of a Swiss barometer, wheeled out in one piece, stand three people: an old man, a young man, and, behind them, a woman —the female, the load-carrier. There is no telling how long they have been watching us. At the first sound of our motor, no doubt, they stepped out from under the trees. Presently they will go back under trees: we feel that about them. In the meanwhile they are not unfriendly—merely, in their way, formal; solemnly formal. The tribesman's reception of the stranger may not be abridged. And as usual, though generation by generation we are forgetting it, these formalities crystallize and hold in reserve the sweet essence of an experience, lost in quick presumption. Here hospitality is almost a tangible thing through which you walk as through the mist of a fall or fountain.

The old man says: "I don't reckon I know yore name."

He could not possibly know it, but there is a tone of noble apology in his voice. One good man should be able to call to mind the patronym of another. He has been remiss. But when I lay in his palm the hard pearl of my name, he and his sons will know themselves richer.

His every statement begins: "I reckon." This, too, is general. You will pull up to a bank, for instance, and shout: "Boys, is there some kind of store up the road yonder?" The answer will come back: "I don't reckon they is." This means: "No, they hain't," and you are expected to interpret it so. The "reckon" has in it no doubt, no irony, no unkindness. It puts into speech an obliqueness which fends off sweaty familiarity, as do certain devices in the talk of Orientals and Red Indians, or, on the Continent, address in the third person. It softens. It is placatingly indirect. It declares that parley will occur in the patriarchal elbow-room of the Testament. In other places and in other ranks it would be called gentlemanly reserve.

The village, when we find it, is a sorry, fly-specked place redeemed for us (its respectable inhabitants might be indignant to hear) by conversations with shanty boat folk at the landing.

Rafe, plump, brown-eyed and Irish, has the born comedian's free tongue and mobile face, his gift for mimicry and oral narrative. Rafe lives in a boat with his "old lady" next door to 'Lige, his "podner" and silent stooge. Rafe was born in Louisville on the river, son and grandson of river men. Himself, he has a mate's "ticket" and has (he says) helped man some of the best boats on the Ohio. Just now, of his own free choice (he says), he is part of no crew, subject to no orders, no schedule, no smothering regularity. He has "never made a dollar on land," and many things will happen to him (among others that he will be damned) before he consents to. Rafe is the lineal descendant of some contemporary of Mike Fink, the Salt River Roarer. Between himself and the common river rat he sees as great difference as between him and "these here big-gut sissies" that come out from offices to fish. His contempt for both is airy.

He is not completely unschooled. He reads *The Saint Louis Post-Dispatch* and has got through, at one time or another, a few books. He admires particularly those of his compatriot and personal friend Mr. Irvin Cobb, into whose *patrie* we are moving—"mouth o' Gar Creek's jest up the line yonder." He has recently heard Mr. Cobb's belled buzzard and is writing to tell him so.

But it is not as an amateur of letters that Rafe distinguishes himself. He is more remarkable as a *raconteur*. He has the correct rich abundance, the flow, the arch silence, the conspiratorial glance, the regard for piquant detail which enables a man to get through the maze of a story as one who chooses stepping stones. And he has the classic understatement, the dry, almost doleful restraint in treating of the hilarious which stamps the American humorist. With accounts of events, trivial as they must appear repeated, he makes us roll in the sand. Thus, only this morning, making his "raise," he stretched out his hand over his dripping catch to pick up a net. A grennel (wholly unprovoked) "ritch" up and sank its teeth into his finger. " 'Y God, boys, I'm hyar t'tell ye thet thar's the first time ever I's *fish-bit*."

Tasting success with this he moves on from anecdote to anecdote—"Hell, one e'enin', I's mate o' the *Risin' Star*," or "Shucks, one mornin', we's just clearin' th' mouth o' Sandy Creek—you's thar wuzn't ye, 'Lige?"

This turning to 'Lige is part of his act, and not the least comic, so does the contrast between them engender mirth. 'Lige is one of our famous "contemporary ancestors," one of the Long Knives of Kentucky. He is nearly seven feet tall, raw-boned, with hook nose and deep-set eyes. He says only: "H-m-m-m," and runs his naked toe into the sand.

Rafe is telling how he fears snakes. 'Y God hit's one varmint he ain't aimin' t'fool with. "One day me'n ole Abe Crenshaw's out under th' willers with a little drinkin' likker—no, beer I think it wuz (I allays aims t'keep pissy-assed drunk when I kin). Abe he had a kind o' *thick-lidded* way o' tawkin', an' he's jest managin' t'say how uncommon few snakes they wuz that side o' the river, when I raised m'bottle fer a snort, an' thar layin' right alongside my cheek wuz a gret big snake wrapped around a willer saplin'—mouth open clean back t'the jints of hit's jaws. Man, I jest cooned right on over th'boat. An' when thet pore Abe seen what wuz on m'mind, he come too. Lit 'bout's fur as from hyar t'the pint. Well, sir, thar we wuz. Boat wouldn't pull out o' th'mud an' the snake wouldn't go away an' the beer a-gettin' hot. Ole John Marmaduke come by in a power boat an' we velled him up er we'd a-ben thar yet."

Rafe is prepared to discuss any locality of the whole countryside. "Take thet shanty-boat settlement up on Pigeon Creek. God damn now, thar's a murderous hole! Even steal from one another! One time me'n 'Lige—we's jest off the *J. T. Harney*—we's aimin' t'buy us a boat out o' th' settlement and not work no more. We's a settin' on a log jest lak we fellers is a-settin' now, restin', jest the least way off, with the settlement in sight, when two fellers come down off the ridge—one of 'em 'ith a star on his chest. He come on up t'me an' he said: "Jes keep on a-settin'." An' his podner says: "Reckon y'all know who we air."

"Reckon yore th' law."

"Whut you fellers up to, hyar?"

"We's aimin' t'buy us a shanty-boat."

"Jes keep yore seat. We're a-huntin' skinned hawg* and one o'them boats is a-goin' t'be fer sale."

"Well, sir, we kep a-settin' an' a-watchin'. The law went a runnin' through first one boat an' then another an' th'ole sheriff his chin wuz jest a-draggin'. Seem lak he's a findin'

*Hog stolen by shanty-boat people, killed and dressed out at once so that the owner of the animal, should he call, would be unable to identify it.

skinned hawg in ev'y damned one o' them boats. That didn't prove nothin' cause course he's jest a-huntin' fer *one.*"

Rafe is acquainted with the jails and officers of all the towns about. He sees it as inevitable that a healthy man and "justice" should make war upon one another. Take the town of Cave-in-Rock, for instance—"hit's *bad,* man, and hit's ben *bad,* sence th'beginnin' o' time." There it seems Rafe was once "th'owed in jail fur some little thing that didn't matter," and the magistrate refused to sign an order for his release. Rafe was not upset, because he has lots of friends in Cave-in-Rock—"course they's all good Americans: Joe Maronek and Tony Siciliano." It was Mr. Siciliano who, in person and by physical force, escorted the magistrate into Rafe's presence for the signing of necessary documents. "I don't reckon the boys handled him any too careful. He didn't look right neat time they'd got him into the jailhouse."

But Cave-in-Rock is a Sabbath School compared to Cairo. There 'Lige and Rafe and Kentucky Red and Choctaw Tom have, miraculously, survived many an evening's entertainment. The women in Cairo especially, Rafe thinks, are plumb mean. A whore-lady whom you meet in a bar and who leaves with you the impression that you have an engagement with her, may at any moment seize your money and rush for the door. "An' if you foller her y'ain't goin' t'make any fu'ther'n the street. No, sir: right thar's whar yo're conked by her reg'lar *es*cort. Happened t'Red once. He got well but hit wuz a God's wonder."

"As fur fightin' and scrappin', hit goes on all th'time in Cairo. They hain't no in*dus*try thar. Town makes hits livin' off arrests. Course they's awful God damned *sweet* about it [gesture of gentleman accepting a *petit four*]: they won't tetch ye less they know yo're off a right good boat. Pud, he's the constable, he'd say: 'Bill, is 'Lige an' Rafe off anything?' Knowed damn well we had a stake, y'understand, er he'd a said: 'Whyn't you bastards git out'n the alley'n kill one another?'"

From Rafe's landing we set out in a panorama as great as those we left on the Mississippi. The Ohio is high, abnormally high for summer. At Dam 53, where usually we should pass through a lock, there is no sign of dam or lock. Everything is under water. We camp once more, tired by current and wind and light, having as little sleep by the ringing surf as one gets in the village hotel, in a room too close to the courthouse clock.

And this morning there is heat again, and blinding rhinestone water. The wind has quieted a little so that, there being no white caps, we are conscious again of the westward-drilling current. Yet of yesterday's agitation there is still some sign. From moment to moment a section of river, as broad as the lot on which your house is built, rises from the general level, sighs, and drops. Lifted on one of these we look down about us. We descend with the pleasure of children playing in hay. Enormously high above us, in a sky as blue as Western skies, there ride clouds, skidding off rapidly in a wind that is not a wind

of earth. Fast as they go they throw a shade. Sometimes
we balance in an island of that shade, looking out as from
a leafiness into light. We at one terminus of the cool
beam, with the cloud at the other, feel a curious intimacy
with the cloud, a curiously exultant knowledge of the
space in which clouds move, and, beyond them, the astral
bodies. To the individual man, in such moments, is possible a weightless detachment from himself, an issuance,
as in early religious painting the soul is seen leaving the
body as a little vapor. Human life as it is usually lived
seems now an act to be watched as a child stands by at a
street fight, sickened. The planter who seeds and reaps
and dampens his finger to find the wind; the herdsman
who rises at night to read stars; the hunter, the fisher, the
sailor who holds his wheel against a swell—these seem
reasonable. But the ambitious in commerce and politics,
the aggressive in war, all who shut themselves from planets
and the weather of space, they are dangerous and obscene.
The academic in art and philosophy, too, one must hold
no part with; they blink like the toad dislodged alive—
but barely—from the wall of an Inca dwelling.

Seeing before us a bridge that spans the river, finding
from the map that we are approaching the town of Metropolis, we gather ourselves and our effects as do folk
who mean shortly to get down from a train. With all
our experience we can still be fooled by tricks of distance.
It is not within that hour or within the next or the next
that we reach the town. There is in the meanwhile the

diversion of watching passing boats, the *Golden Eagle* and the *H. L. Roberts.* In a far bend they turn to disappear, dark, their detail gone, but with the stern wheel white as a rabbit's tail. Until afternoon we struggle constantly against the current, reaching dock less exhausted by work than by deceived expectation.

Beyond Metropolis one may halt to examine the faint trace of Fort Massac, built by the French in 1758, as they fell back from their defeat at Fort Duquesne. The date seems far, but at that time these men had already, and long ago, become acquainted with the Ohio. There seems to be no question that, about 1670, La Salle descended to the "falls" at the site of Louisville. And there is definite record of the voyage of Bienville, who came in 1749 to forestall the claims of Virginians who had been clamoring for land. Here he brought his Canadians, with the "heavy stalking of mediæval soldiery into the pages of modern history," dropping lead tablets at the mouth of tributaries, claiming for his king, in 1749, land on which, in 1849, men would be turning out for American house-raisings, fish-fries, elections.

Here on the ruins of the fort stands a statue of George Rogers Clark, who began in the vicinity his march upon Kaskaskia. He is shown as we like to picture our pioneer ancestors; a glorious buckskin boy, perfect captain for the small college football team, except that he has on his face the light of conscious destiny. He belongs to those days of few imponderables, when the nation's stint was merely conquest: when an individual, with good elimination and manly daring, was adequate. Clark may well have had on his face the expression of this bronze. And no American yet whose past goes back to the wilderness world of 1778 (and who has therefore the horn-call of an old nostalgia in him) would fail to follow a boy with such manhood on him; to follow him even out to the prairies of eight-foot grass, to woods so deep that even the guides confessed they were "bewildered."

From Fort Massac there is visible shortly another bridge, marking this time the approaches to Paducah. Past this and to the town itself Kentucky preserves her savage quiet, so that the town, once reached, gives the impression of an outpost. Behind the levee is a small modern city which might be anywhere else in the South or Middle West; but the levee itself, sloping down from an old esplanade overlooking the confluence of the Ohio and the Tennessee, has so deeply the imprint of the past that we remember the outpost, not the city.

It is almost sunset as we turn up the mouth of the Tennessee, passing huddles of boats, some in good shape, others mouldering and barely afloat, having the look of objects abandoned in an attic. Not all of them, however, are uninhabited.

Uncertain if we are on the main body of the river, we pull up to a tumbledown fish boat to ask. On the back "porch" sits a girl, her bare feet on the wet floor. One full breast is exposed to view; she takes hold of it as if it were not a part of her body, thrusting it under her dress.

In her lap lies a male baby, naked. To our question: "Are we on the Tennessee River, ma'am?" she answers softly: "This is hit." At that moment the father comes on board. The girl smiles, not lifting her head as he halts, drawing a finger over the baby's belly. For a moment his head is against hers. They are hardly more than children. Yet the woman is already wife and mother, living for her men. The boy is husband and father, offering with his virility the fish he takes. The two of them handle dimes and coppers as they would cut stones, because the coin and the gem are rare. They live on this craft, so water-logged that bits of the soft wood remain beneath your nails.

The Tennessee, here where it flows into the Ohio, is visibly a Southern stream. In fact, profound and slow in this low country, it is more suggestive of the Deep South than it will be later in the sun of the uplands. Like the Cumberland, the Tennessee serves as entrance to a land lightly tinted on the map showing density of population. It is a region smelling of wood smoke, a region of houses having dog runs and galleries where patchwork quilts are hung to air. For miles there is only the meekest village by way of settlement. Below Florence, in Alabama, there is no good-sized town: until Chattanooga, no city. For the casual traveller, keeping in motion, with no time to uncover the mildew of human distress, these miles are an uninterrupted enchantment. He will live mornings of mist and then of clarity so great that in it objects stand like gnats in amber; days of sun and wind when water is whipped to the color of Western sage, folding into slow waves that stretch as do cats when they put forth their paws and yawn. He will have evenings when hawks are mewing, when little fish leap, the while ashore are fireflies in the sway of ripening grain. He will waken of nights when silence like a tent collapsed lies over him; that will be the time when timid things are out, when mud of the water hole oozes from the cleft hoof and tongues are put from whiskered mouths.

There will be men about, to be sure, but with the proportion in which you might like to see deer. They are not rich men. Economically their woes date back to the War Between the States and, beyond, to the days when their fathers moved from the set structure of East coast society. Yet only the unwise would be moved to too much pity. If some of these folk rarely feel in their hands the weight of cash they have unknowingly, in the midst of world drought, kept a spiritual humidity which makes of them the real victors.

Setting aside for the moment their fine (if sometimes unwilling) freedom from gadgets and the machine: setting aside their religion which, if it is the hymn-bawling and doctrinal squabble represented in the newspapers, supports at least the patriarchal pattern of the family and, among a whole folk, keeps alive the poetry of hart and waterbrook: setting aside those things, consider for the moment the survival among these people of early American democracy. In the post office of the village of Savannah I am delayed for long by an old man. He has a deep eye, an aquiline nose and tobacco-stained moustache; his fingers are twisted over the head of his cane. Angrily he tells the clerk through the grilled window what the "people" will stand and what they won't. Angrily he stamps out, his voice and his cane leaving echo. He could easily be made comic. Yet he is in his living presence a principle which we usually inspect in the form of a cupola, a width of floor board, a dimension of glass in colonial buildings preserved by the D. A. R. He would have talked eagerly to my grandfather; to my grandfather who, thrusting out his beard, used to tell me of his first vote; how he rode on that day to the county seat and back sitting his horse very straight. "I was," he would say to me, *"a citizen of the Republic!"* At that age I could not be sure what a citizen was, or a republic. But his voice set up a vibration in me which is still there. His statement is now one with those I recall from Cicero, in the language of which I know so little but which mystically is mine along with English and first milk. The Southerner who, even in these frightening days, does not grow solemn at the mention of Latin may be marked for a traitor.

The Tennessee, though not a small stream, will be more intimate than the greater rivers. We do not, as on the Ohio, feel safer in the wide midstream. Here we may "trim willows"—that is, keep close to shore—and so re-enter the life of earth. A speedboat makes for us from upstream, splitting with its prow a symmetrical heart of spray. It goes down toward Paducah, carrying with it the last hint of town. A young duck, overtaken in an inlet, lifts his wings and "walks" to shore. A small blue heron on a log beside us turns his head this way and that, taking off only when he must. He is as typical of that bank as in other lands the ibis and the nightingale.

As dusk begins to thicken we are forced to think of camp, and make for a height that has a clearing in the brush beneath the trees. As we strike gravel we are halted, with the amazement we should feel to hear a *Te Deum* intoned from the woods. It is not a sound that stops us, nor any physical barrier in the way. It is an odor. An odor as compelling as the milkiness of babies' breath, the perfume of wild berry beds. It is the smell of corn. There must be lying behind the grove acre on acre of it, all ripe. Somewhere close are thousands of ears full of juice, perspiring under blond silk. The still air is a perfect carrier. A man blind and deaf in our tent tonight would say: "There is fire at hand, and water and corn." We who see and hear should add: "There are hounds and owls. On the river, Venus the planet and a navigation light have each a long reflection."

We are wakened at five by the *Jayhawker*, moving upstream with coal. She disappears at the bend, kicking water into light which falls upon her as she clears the frigid shade.

We dress and push off quickly, begrudging even time for coffee. With air brushing knee-cap and navel and throat, such mornings are as moving to us as the first morning. There are no second and third mornings: no twenty-fifth, no thirty-seventh. All are initial. The woodwind monotone of doves, the dipping of boughs to the river, the purity of air, the depth of water and its strength; these and the sense of freedom given by sun on my head, by wind feeling over the flesh of my belly, these are possessed as if for the first time, tremulously, after a night of doubt. It is not without sacrifice that I have come here; not without refusal to compromise; without renunciation of much called necessary. But now, like the crackbrained inventor running from his laboratory yelling: "God! God! See! It works!" I could make from the tent. But there is no question of such demonstration. There are one's companions before whom even naked one is restrained. Secretly I am grateful to them when, tensely, they answer my tense remarks; when they hurry with my haste to pack; when they look back with me, as if expecting pursuit. Their hearts, too, are being lipped, nibbled by this prehensile glee: the departing, the always leaving in birdsong and mist.

Below the village of Birmingham we come upon an island three miles long. Passing to leeward we enter a narrow channel, dark and completely arched by trees. To either side is a jungle into which we cannot see. Our view is straight ahead: branches immediately at hand silhouetted against blue distance, with, under the blue, water of the channel leaping like the backs of sheep.

Birmingham is tiny and inoffensive. In its first building we stop for beer, mingling with a line of ragged men. One of them is summoned presently by a sun-bonnetted

woman who calls from the door: "Pa, you git on home!"
To the company she observes dispassionately: "He loves
that stuff more'n a hawg loves slop."

In the grocery store we are waited upon by an old
proprietor with dim blue eyes and somnambulist's manner. He is afraid he has not much to offer. Perhaps not,
but more than most. In many hamlets I find these and
nothing else for sale: snuff, canned vienna sausages, wormy
raisins, sugar and coffee. No vegetables. A grocer whom
I asked for onions spoke for them all when he said:
"What'd I be doin' with onions? Folks *raises* stuff like
that."

As I gather my purchases to leave, I find standing behind me a pretty but very dirty little girl. She is holding
upward in her palm one egg. She has come from her home
to the store to sell it. Pushing the grocer aside, represent-
ing myself to be in great need of an egg, I give her five
cents. She curtsies, remembering to say, "Thank you indeed, sir." Rural America is, in America, the last desperate retreat of good manners.

Back at the landing we find two youths. One is black.
He seems to have no bones in his gangling body. His
wrists and ankles protrude a great way from his overalls.
On his head he has a ragged felt hat, like the husk of
a bean seed come upward on the sprout. He reminds me
of my house-boy at home who, loyally and deftly, taking
gratitude for granted, surrounds me with ease. Moreover,
obscurely, my blood remembers him. For over two hundred years I have known this rascal. Therefore I deign

to say: "Hi, boy." His mouth has been open to answer this greeting. "Yassuh," he says joyously, "yassuh. How do?" He remembers me too, obscurely, and knows that as I should cherish a blooded setter I should cherish him— tolerating no ill-bred foolishness. Later, when we are ready to push off, he approaches me, saying: "Boss man, y'all ben raised with black folks: ain' dat right?" "Nigger boy," I answer solemnly, flashing him, man to man, a look of gratitude, "that I have."

The second lad is white, therefore less free with us. But when he has received our formal denial that we have any connection whatever with the *law*, his hunger to talk overcomes him.

"I hain't never ben in jail nor in court," he says, "it'd skeer the livin' pee out o' me."

When I suggest that if I *were* the law, and if he were innocent, he would have no need to fear me:

"That hain't got nuthin' t'do with hit. Lots o'them boys a-layin' up in prison hain't done a God's blessed thing."

He regards all convicts (especially those in the death row) as Robin Hoods. The injustice of it burns his heart, and more than the injustice, horror of confinement, of restriction. For this reason he has also a lively distaste for the army.

"I druther be in hell with m'back broke than t'go off to the war. They don't keer how they treat a feller once they git him in the troops."

It is not that a hearty up-and-above-board free-for-all would not appeal to him. He does not mean that he is

170

not courageous. He is trying to tell me that he has a frantic fear of being manœuvred into a trap where some other man can *tell him what to do*. And I, whose racial background is the same as his, need make no great effort to understand. To give our lives for our country is one thing—desirable, if life must be given. *Pro patria mori*, for the boy and me and our kind, is an epitaph to strive for. But to cancel individuality in ranks; to stand and march; to receive orders snapped by a fellow who thereby (in our estimation) would become an inferior—that is another thing. The order of the officer would be obeyed, but in our hearts a Southern voice would be repeating: "Kain't air man tell me what to do!" And in a sense no man would be telling us what to do. The part of us that might matter to a god or our brother would remain unhindered as a leaping fish. If this boy and I are to be fighters, the best would be to give us a leader whom we could love, to whom it would become important to remain loyal; then, if possible, keep us out of close ranks. Tell us to get out on the Murfreesborough Road and not let nobody by. We should go then to the Murfreesborough Road. If a man got by, his pants would be smoking.

To bring the talk into other channels I remark that the boy is lucky to be living on the Tennessee; that it is a lovely stream. I am certain that this language will irritate him. And sure enough he answers: "Aw balls." He would have me know that he was born in a shanty boat on the Mississippi and that he hain't ben out of sight of water since. He hates it. What he wants is a red automobile and plenty of gas. How should *I* like it in winter with ice cakes a-shovin' agin the boat an' the wind a-howlin' an' the water a-comin' up? His anger rises to such height that it becomes lyric. I see that the lad, contrary to what he imagines, loves the river very much; that when he exchanges it for the red automobile, he will be a sick and disorientated boy.

From Birmingham we move up slowly through the hot afternoon, zigzagging so as to keep in the scroll of shade cast by the wood. We camp in a kind of shallow bay—wakened at daybreak by a whirr of wings at the door and about the walls of the tent. At first light the birds come to clean what we put aside at dinner, to peck at the skillets and plates we left in the dark. We step naked into cold fog; air in our lungs marks their boundary as with a razor. In all North America three things are clear: a strip of beach, a twisted young cypress tree and, at its foot, a frog whose wink involves the whole face. These things are seen as they are not in full light; each small leaf of the cypress is brilliant green, stiff and fragile; the frog too is wet green, his eye is bright; the beach is yellow. Its gravel is loose, giving off a sound as of large beads under our weight. All this exists in a cavity of fog: a world small and ardent, remote as peaked crystals in a hollow rock. Beyond, we see nothing. The river is a sound, not a sight, though it flows by the fire that burns before us, unnaturally yellow. Driftwood passes, horizontal, as on air. But the *fiat lux* of the day has been pronounced, and before our eyes is enacted a Genesis-without-Eve. The east, opposite, glows as if from a depth within, sulphur and pearl. Earth and water stand apart. Creatures of land and air and the stream sing and leap. A man comes down the river in a boat. We hear the well-bucket thud of his oars; then, as large fish may be seen through ice, we make out his body—the round of his back as he leans forward, the point of his elbows as he draws back. He calls out: "Hi, Unc' Henry!" mistaking our flame in the mist for another.

Above Birmingham rises a line of hills, backing the timber. As if its way were hewn through gateway and gateway the river turns, bordered by trees exact and tall. We pass increasing numbers of shell fishermen. They are drifting slowly, sinking the rod of brails—lines from which hang four coarse hooks that irritate the mussel and make him close his shell about their prongs. Sometimes we find the men ashore in "camps" where, having sorted them, they "boil out" mussels in vats over a fire in a trench. The shells, afterward, are stacked in pens which resemble pig sties though they smell much worse. Later they will be purchased by men of a boat from Paducah, sent by the button factories. The shells have endless categories, varying like the nomenclature of fish from region to region, and with subdivisions beyond my ken: "sheep ears," "lady fingers," "pig toes," "warty backs" and the rare "sand shell" for which one gets a best price of eighty dollars a ton.

Our outfit makes an object of great interest to such a

fisherman. He is stern as an Indian until we speak or
wave. Then, if the rod of brails is down and his hands are
busy, he ducks his head in vigorous nods. When he can
bring the rod up he waves, too late, but eager not to be
thought uncivil. Nearly all are friendly if one is not
abrupt; if one acquires patience to go through the cere-
mony of introduction so like the meeting of strange dogs
that at first one is apprehensive lest it be carried too far.
If the men are not friendly it is that they are timid, or
actually frightened. Once, when we turned quickly (too
quickly) for the shade of a bay a young fellow, whose
boat was moored there, caught hold of a branch above him,
leapt to the bank, disappeared among the trees and stood
nervously treading leaves until we went away. "Ye don't
never want to corner a feller like that," a man told us
later. "He mought have his reasons."

Very rarely are there women in the shell "camps." And
if no men are by we pass them with a curt nod. It is an
error on the part of the stranger to greet otherwise the
lone woods woman. Under the age of eighty, if she is
decent, she expects to preserve the silence of a squaw in
the presence of a man she does not know. He is not simply
a stranger, he is a male; his sex has a sheen as of feathers.
No one, without sufficient knowledge of the terrain to
elude a posse, had better insist. But it is seldom that we
see women. This water and its banks make a men's world.
Often, in the shade of the "camps," the boys work naked.
And their classic question as we approach: "Got any women
with ye?" Sometimes, while we are still too far away for

the call, through the glasses I can see the whole "camp" bent in the motion of men who put on trousers. Many of them have the bodies of college oarsmen; some are even taller and more vigorous, so that in town clothes they would inevitably be comic. After weeks, however, of witnessing their naturalness and strength, it is plain that the gentleman in claw-hammer tails and striped trousers is not, after all, a model: he is a creature whom we have come to tolerate slowly. Whether in detail the bodies are fine or not, the sight of unharnessed white flesh among the leaves and in the light that falls between the leaves is good. Oddly it seems something you remember, if not with your brains, then with the marrow of your bone.

We ascend the east bank grazing thickets of ironwood and birch, sweet gum and cypress still, afternoon, giving extravagantly of their cool. They are so dense that the sun never shines among them fully. In an opening of the vines that trail from them, sometimes, from the blank glare of outer light, we have a thumbnail glimpse into the chill inside—a golden warbler fluttering; a heron holding a frog that has conceded victory. The river, this far from its mouth, has shaken off whatever it may have had of commonplace. It flows with good speed, the force distributed evenly over its breadth. At a given point, precisely, here and there it breaks into ripples; beyond that line it is polished, so still that the shell boats seem elevated on their own reflections. Dwellings begin to appear, but they are for the most part cabins in a scanty patch of corn. This

is a region of which one could say that it was halted in
the process of pioneering by the brutalities of War and
Reconstruction.

We try, and find it very difficult, to locate the site of
Fort Henry. We consult a bearded ancient who stands
barefoot in the three inches of water that pave his boat.
A way off he looks forbidding. His beard and consecrated
gestures in handling fish give him the dignity of prophets.
But close up the beauty of his old eyes inspires a confidence; he is gentle with the gentleness of certain game
birds—grouse and prairie hens—that let themselves be
stoned.

"Fort Henry? There ain't anything at Fort Henry now.
The breastworks *wuz* marked with a stone. Reckon hit
mought be in the river now. Hit had U. S. cut into hit,
an' the owners of the land mebbe wuzn't right certain
they wanted t'have anything t'do with that gov'mint."

But he gives us directions enough that finally, in the
wilt of afternoon heat, we find what is left of the fort.
Part of it is dense with weeds. Part lies under corn. Like
a man overcome with sleep who strives to remain alert,
remembering danger, I try to realize what I am seeing.
Here from the water swords are dredged; and here, in
the field, bullets are washed out by the rains. Today is
hot. The doves are monotonous and make one sleepy.
Under the yellow rosebush of cabin yards, hens scratch in
the dust, holding out their wings, saying: "Caw-w-wk?
caw-w-w-wk? cawk?" But once it was February and there
was flood and gloom. The Union boats stood out in the

river, panting with the way that steamboats have. They had brought Grant's men. The air was bruised and dark and quick with the scarlet dots of firing guns. Fort Henry fell. Grant went overland the miles to Donelson. The fleet, returning to the Ohio, moved up the Cumberland to meet him before Donelson. And Donelson was taken. Middle Tennessee was lost to us. Kentucky was lost to us. And shade fell over a church called Shiloh.

Leaving this scene, passing again the bearded one who holds up his hand to call out something he had forgot ("Pa was there!"), we move on to a night's camp at the upper end of Sandy Island. Here the river is split, entering to the right a main channel; to the left, a smaller one. We are placed in an acre or so of gravel which "flows" with the grace left on it by water of the last flood. Facing the lesser channel it is as if we were, say, on the Current River of the Missouri Ozarks. The water is swift and clear over a gravel bottom; the beach is hard and clean; the canoe dawdles in a little bay thrashing with minnows. In a dead tree opposite we count more than thirty buzzards, quaintly spaced. Some droop motionless; others sidle foot by foot along a branch, neck and wing outstretched, like parrots. The sight of them would return my mind to the battle at Fort Henry, but my boys, being boys, have together one idea. The only piece of baggage unpacked for a time is a rifle. For long the air is filled with buzzards. But they return, furtively, by the moon; against its light the high-shouldered silhouettes are plain.

## Where the Rivers Meet

When we have bathed in the frigid water we come back nude over the gravel to sleep, through air I should have said is still, but which moves over my skin with a magic of small variations. Zippered in my sleeping bag, hooded in my parka, I am sheltered from the cold of night and, more or less, from mosquitoes. I am very snug. More so yet when I look up. The rim of my hood and around it, close, the circle of woods, make a peephole into interstellar space. It is as if in a cave I should sit beneath a hole rotted out of the roof. While I watch, stars that have been there long give way and fall: it happens that I, on my back in the sand, witness the end. All, those that drop and those that stay to glitter, seem within reach of my arm. An owl flying over thrusts them away again. The beam of my vision which had seemed short, intercepted by his known littleness, lengthens the incalculable miles.

With rain threatening, we remain a day in this camp. Mist rolls over the hills to the south. Upstream the water is ink-blue, like the sky. The line of woods at its shore is green as if seen through a bottle; the white tail of passing steamers is very, very white. These things lie in the hush preceding storm, in the cleared air, with the hair-raising precision of objects seen in dream—the dream that recurs when you drop off again, having wakened to assure yourself it is not so. It is at once dramatic and oppressive. We are restless. The buzzards rise in twos and threes, circle their tree, and light. They stare morosely. From time to time one turns her head and flabby neck to stare long into the face of one beside her on the roost.

# The Ohio and the Tennessee

On the second morning after our arrival here it has
not rained, nor has the sky changed. Therefore we set
out, our nose of honest American spruce white in the blue
water as a brazen prow in an ancient sea. So to the landing of the village of Danville. Here we are met by a
ferryman, naked to the waist. His backbone is sunk like
the spine of a draft horse. His shoulders are mighty and
exquisitely muscled. But he is not brutish. His voice is
startlingly low, like a bow-length off the C string of a
'cello, muted. There is fantastic contrast between his anvil
strength and the bashful blue kindliness of his glance as
he gives us directions.

In the village I step the worn boards of the grocery
store gallery between two lines of chairs and benches.
They are occupied by men too old to work or who, left
idle by threat of weather, have gathered here to chat.
They move back their plough shoes as I approach. They
are dead quiet, examining me impersonally as they would
peer into crevasses made by an earthquake. When I am
once inside, with the undertone men use around a corpse,
they begin to talk about me:

"He's right slim."

"Y'all see he had on Indian shoes?"

"I told you I kep' hearin' a furrin motor, Ned, you
damned old fool."

They are mute again as I emerge. It hurts my heart
whenever, as now, I have not time to thaw such people
out, to make them admit we are nearer kin than they
supposed. Whether city men like me or not is never im-

179

portant. Until countrymen smile it is as if a dog or child had shied. Fortunately now the grocer appears in the door, waving a handful of dollar bills:

"Mister, you left yore change! An' me 'ith all that trouble to make hit! Boys," he turns jovially to the gallery, "this here ain't no Yankee."

This opinion, and my indignation at the sentence without a hearing, breaks the ice. Now they may ask me what they are burning to know:

"Son, from the look o' yore hands, y'ain't off no work boat?"

"Air you boys fishin'?"

"You fellers a-sellin' Bibles?"

"Reckon you boys'd be from Padooky?"

"Then whar at did y'all start?"

The answer to this last brings wide-eyed smiles.

"Is that a fact?"

"Now did ye jest turn right out o' the Mississippi into the . . ."

"Be dogged if it ain't like the ole days."

I start off again, accompanied by two little niggers who prance and stamp and kick up dust, chanting: "Indian slippahs! Indian slippahs!" until I say: "Here, you pickaninnies, pack these jugs!" They dart forward, each taking a gallon thermos, marching ahead of me, happy as if I had dealt out banners to carry in wind.

Back on the river we put in hours of threading islands, diamond-shaped, finger-shaped, amorously grown to the water line with cane, covered inland with forest trees. At a distance such isles, lying exactly on their own reflections, seem to soar like fountains, free and slow. They have nothing static. They are troubling as the doves and the thrush that sing out of them over the water from under leaves.

In bursts of sun that appear and wilt us and fade, we pass the *Bedford* of Paducah. She is moored below a "camp." Men dressed, half-dressed and undressed, down from among the trees, are bringing bushels of shells that roll with the sound of so many hailstones. There sits forward, under a yellow beach umbrella, a boss in a white helmet. He weighs, records, and deals out money. Afterward, as we ascend the river ahead of the *Bedford*, people will ask: "How much are they payin'?" And their wonder that we do not know will be less great than ours that they think we might. We are all but literally lost, cut off from daily life of any land. And we are increasingly intoxicated by an awareness that it does not matter if we are lost. On a bar near the landing for Johnsonville a lad wishes to know where we are from. To make it simpler I answer that we are all from Saint Louis.

"Saint Louis? Is that up the river, or down?"

Saint Louis, I tell him, is neither up nor down the Tennessee. It is a city to the northwest on the Mississippi. But my voice by this time is as full of doubt as his. To me, too, it begins to seem unlikely that one could be from Saint Louis. He has given me, in mid-afternoon, the sensation I have at night, leaning back to find the Dipper.

Feeling need to explain to some one that for weeks stars and the wind have made doorjamb and sill of my house, I tell it to this boy. He answers, looking down at his hands:

"I know. When a man's ben sleepin' out at night, ain't no room fit to hold him."

Beyond the bridge of the Memphis-Nashville highway (spanking clean and silver against the angry blue of the sky) we are forced to put to shore in a poor emergency camp. There is high wind, then silence; then the air, for thirty minutes, is solid with rain. We have made no ditch about the tent. It is unwisely situated on a slope. It and everything in it is wet. At bedtime, during a lull, we back out of it in disgust. It is slimy and smells bad. To stand in it gingerly a while—perhaps: but to lie down in it—no. We should prefer (so we imagine now!) to stand out the night in cold water to our necks. On a narrow margin of slanting gravel, between high ground and water, we spread our sleeping bags. They are wet outside. Inside, they are a miracle of dry warmth. Watching blurred stars, hearing the roll of thunder and halloos for a ferryman upstream, I drop to sleep.

At a quarter past two I am wakened by a vigorous pounding on my chest.

"Get up! Quick! Look!"

There is no need to get up or to look. I do not have to push investigation far to know that my sleeping bag, from my hips down, is floating; that, this time, it is soaked through and through. While we slept the river rose. It was, in fact, made to rise. Far upstream water has been let out from Pickwick Dam. Now our boat, moored once at our feet, is far out. The river is hitting everywhere about us, sucking, kissing. It has more than forward motion. Our beds are wet. The tent is wet (and sour with mildew). We are naked. Our moccasins feel as if for weeks they have been rotting with stems in a vase. The air is beaded with drizzle. There is therefore one thing, and one thing only, to do. We are gay. Breaking open logs for dry wood, we sit about the fire drinking coffee. We are weak, before long, with real mirth. When at daylight the last of the fire sizzles out in rising water, we get up to put on clothing, wet as if it had purposely been lowered in water. A swimmer is dispatched for the canoe. Clammy, muddy-toed, trembling, we toss into it baggage usually packed with care. So, with no breakfast, without promise of lunch we set out upstream.

There are intermittent hard showers that blot out sight, sending streams of rain down the neck of our ponchos. The poncho was designed—be sure of it—by some blunt enemy of campers, to canalize the water that falls on a man; to make sure that, between his vestigial breasts, it will flow swiftly to his stomach, his crotch, leaving a cold pool on the waterproof cushion beneath him. We are filthy. We do not like the way we smell. We are shuddering with goose flesh. We are not sure when we shall be able to find food, or how it can be cooked. And, miracles aside, where shall we lay our heads tonight?

In the face of these facts, these questions, we spend a morning—one could not call it charming; it is *charmed*. In a sharp southeast bend the hills to the east, until now barely visible, crowd to the bank. Behind these others rise, with suggestion of mountains, in four levels. A fifth, the misty last, can be made out with glasses. On some shoulder of this range the sun drops, cleaving fog, bright as one dreams in the dark that light is bright, fading, leaving us in a green and sulphur dusk as on some day of great eclipse. Between showers come pockets of beaded silence, muffled, shut off by rain that is leaving and rain coming. The only sound is the sound, as of rapid skirts, of flying birds. Over us cuts a notched and veteran hawk. Ducks go by, level and systematic, as if on routine business. The sentimental doves come down to rocks to drink, clean in the wet, elegant among the fluted cones of cypress root. Beyond us often, below a line exact, the river dissolves not quite in rapids, but in a speedy crinkling. This portion seems an incline sloping upward toward the rim, the hairline beyond which the river once more is black and still, reflecting with such scruple that even with glasses land and the soul of land on water mingle.

At the mouth of Duck River, coming in from the east, there is some agitation; both streams are swollen and the meeting is difficult. Opposite their junction rides a buoy. Like a live thing bitten and pulled under, it struggles and flails; sinks and rises not quite breaking water; sinks and shoots back high as if squeezed from a sheath, to fall in foam. At Sycamore Landing near by we stop and talk with the men of the mailboat which, wallowing and white-lipped, arrives behind us, siren screaming because we have taken its usual place. A farmer-fisherman who comes up admits that the water is "dingy" after last night's rise. He thinks it would be best for us to pull over and spend the day with him. This I refuse to do. The level guilelessness of his eye proclaims him rich in a way; he is otherwise poor. He would kill his last pullet to feed us.

The village of Perryville passed, we are threatened by long and heavy rain once more. We camp on the tilted shelves, and among the rounded elephant rocks of a ruined bluff. Lizards rattle out of the grass. Birds descend from air, altering their course abruptly when they see us. The ground is covered with persimmons, purple as grapes, fallen before season. Much would interest us if we could remain out. But a meal is to be got in haste. Before it can be eaten, rain falls. Dark closes in, and we are forced to the tent. For a moment we revolt and gaiety fails. The tent is mildewed and gummy: it smells like a latrine. Our beds are like discarded diapers. But it is this or a night in pelting rain on rock. We lie with bared teeth, waiting for fatigue and body heat to work their wonder.

Morning alternates bright heat and gloom of swollen-bellied cloud. We wake hearing wings through the tent, and oarlocks of the punctual fishermen. Ahead of us the river comes on, out of hills and forest, hills and forest, deep and vigilant.

Having no longer, as far as rain is concerned, reason to

185

go forward or back, to stand or sit, we set off doggedly for a day of islands—islands hung so thick with vine that it is not possible to see to what the vine is clinging. Now, more than in the space of mid-Mississippi, we feel cut off. Heart into heart beyond heart we have got into webby solitude where travellers rarely go, where we ourselves will leave no print when our wake has reached the shore. Before us a heron flies and, as we approach his perch, flies on. The wet branch gives with his weight. Drops fall to prick his reflection that forms again, broken again as he leaps to leave, scooping his slow way ahead. On the sandy head and end of every island we come upon flocks of herons standing in the shallows, in the coarse grass. They look at us foolishly and at one another "dumbfounded as a cow before a new gate" and do not fly. They are our only companions.

Before evening we sight the village of Clifton. It sits on hills with a road winding up from the ferry. The *Riverside Hotel* and the "store blocks" beyond it have so well the tone of things *ante-bellum* that, pictured, they could pass in a collection of Brady. It is true that, once afoot in the main street, there are details which correct this impression. There is, for instance, a beauty shoppe. But, directly at its entrance is stretched, in the pink of form, a sow. She opens and closes her blond-lashed eyes. She mutters to herself and lets her breasts roll where they will, like the coarse member of a refined family, who will be damned if she puts on airs for company.

# The Ohio and the Tennessee

The banker and merchants of the place are better contained. They turn over and over in their fingers—and ultimately refuse to accept—our travellers' checks. They have never seen, or with fine canniness profess never to have seen, such things. They are of the type of small businessman who will mortgage his shoes to buy gold bricks from a crook in a cocked fedora: honesty in moccasins he knows at once for a villain. Our disgust is warmly shared by a laiety that crowds to the door of a given shop, following us to the next, to know the outcome. As we leave the last, a man pulls at my sleeve:

"Why, them sons of bitches! Boy, if I had a nickel in cash, hit'd be yore'n."

This is doubtless sincere. Out beyond town I could find farm wives to heap vegetables in my basket, saying: "Give me what you want fer'em, son; or take 'em fer nothin'." And there was lately the fisherman, honestly regretting that I would not spend the day in his cabin (empty as a sentry box), eating food he had earned "pulling" mussels.

We leave therefore without rancor, but also with no food. For dinner we choose among cans that for days have been rolling in the bottom of the boat and have no longer their labels. In this way a menu may be composed which makes up in surprise what it lacks in à propos.

Camp tonight is on a bar with long slope to the woods. It is this gradual incline that saves us. After bed I hear the sound I have come to know. The water is rising. Tomorrow the tufts of grass on the lower beach will just protrude, making a duck terrain. The hummock around which I walked to bathe will be in its own right an island, with current flowing from its downstream point.

Beyond this place the bluffs rise close. They are so high, so little exists to give them scale, that there is no clue to their size until one sights the dot of a shellboat beneath their base of rock. The river to the other side is invariably hemmed by woods. Before us and behind, it is shut off with bends so that often we have, as on a lake, miles of water where the "v" from the prow moves out to meet the "v" of the wake. Merged and faint the slow roll reaches shore.

At the landing of Saltillo we put in for fuel, tying up by a ferry littered with pickaninnies who stare through the rails but do not dare approach. Two little white boys wade the shallows to look us over. They have the tidiness, the spirit of young gamecocks; but, with that, intelligent eyes, well-set mouths, natural good manners. They are for the moment unhindered by parents, free from school; they do not have to work. Pointing to a fleet of shellboats passing, especially to one boat where there is a lad not more than ten, laboring hard with his father, I ask, "Does his daddy make him do that?"

"No, sir. It's right queer. He jes li-i-ikes it. Kain't nobody understa-a-and that boy."

These two are going fishing. One, while he was waiting for the other to come, has already caught a green trout. Of him I ask the distance to town. He says: "It's over a half, sir."

But his companion protests: "No, Bobby, t'ain't. T'ain't over a quarter from Gibbs's Mill to the cherry tree."

Once more there is in my mind the effect as of sudden stoppage of a wheel. We look at one another in mutual wonder. I the traveller from out the moving river. He the lad whose genial base, in bloom and in frost, is a cherry tree.

By mid-afternoon we have put in at Savannah—the first large village along our way. There are bankers who accept, as a matter of course, checks of the American Express. There are stores which have for sale (along with china nest-eggs and terra cotta string holders shaped like bee hives) fine food nicely presented. There is a Courthouse Square with men loafing, gesticulating over the state of the Union. There is a road leading back to the boat, past old cottages bound by vines to the rock of their chimneys; in the yards are magnolias, crêpe myrtle and box; by the roadside, dusty figs.

At the landing two young farmers approach me. They are freshly shaven and sturdy; their overalls are clean. They live "down in Lawrence County." They are walking to Kansas City, where they are sure of finding jobs. At least they say they are sure. "Lots of railroad gang work is always going on," they explain like men out of the Bible, "in that country." But they are a little tremulous, as if repeating something they have been told and are beginning to doubt. With the dignity of Indians they say that they have no money, that they can persuade neither ferryman nor toll-keeper on the bridge to let them pass, that it is too far to swim. Then one of them pronounces words which my ears scarcely credit. I ask no one else to believe it, but the words, nevertheless, came out on air. The man would like, he says, "to cross over the river and git a little rest in the shade of them trees." They are so near to words I have heard before (and from what lips!) that his image is dimmed before me as I offer my boat. Without this tightened throat I should have given him money also; my sleep for nights to come will be troubled because I forgot. God disgust these lads with the railroad soon, and turn them home out of "that country." Let them know as the Osages knew:

"Acts of touching the earth are divine.
Acts of digging the earth are divine."
And keep them safe at plough in Lawrence County.

Above Savannah, entering a minor channel, we camp on soil we call an island, but which is in effect merely a high spot in the river bed assuming different forms at different water levels. Recently the river has been higher than now. There are all about us wooded mounds, usually oval in shape, that have stood up as islands, growing off this island. In hollows at their base water still lies in pools. There are a great many small fish heads on the sand, a crisscross of heron tracks, and a smell as of cod-liver oil.

This morning we wake to find the reverse of our comedy after nights of sudden rise. This time the river has dropped, or, more properly, been lowered by the gentlemen at Pickwick. We are marooned ashore. The canoe lies on its side, uselessly chained to the leg of a willow. The beach is covered with buzzards, eager for the dying fish, so that they will not fly but retreat before us, hissing protest, hopping as if on crippled feet.

Working fast, we carry the canoe to what is left of our "minor channel," meaning, rather than to portage overland to the main stream, to "walk" our equipment out and up to deeper water. This we do. But our vexation is not ended. The low level has brought bars to the surface and created shoals. The time is gone when we may caper where we please, sure, by the gurgle of our displacement, of safe depth. Twice we run aground with the lower fin of the motor, so that finally, like the steamers, we keep to the marked channel.

Fortunately we have not far to go. In a very short while we pull up to a place one hundred and ninety-eight miles from the mouth of the river—the goal toward which we have been plugging day by day. The spot is called in the table of distances Pittsburg Landing, and marks the eastern limit of the field of Shiloh, now a Federal Military Park. These names are known to me from childhood, along with names of men who fought here: Beauregard, and two that ring like lines of verse—Albert Sidney Johnston, Nathan Bedford Forrest. Here in April of '62 they met Northerners under Grant and Sherman in the first great battle of the War. In such engagements, with masses of untrained boys on both sides, victory (one is told) rests with the army of greater number. So Buell, succeeding in re-enforcing Grant, gave him along with a majority, victory. It was a gain, however, so ragged and so dearly bought that even Sherman advised against pursuit. The Confederacy, seeing what was indeed only withdrawal after valorous fight, was encouraged.

Immediately above the landing is the park headquarters, surrounded by Union graves (our men lie in trenches off to the west) under ivy, under magnolia, under juniper silver-blue with berries. Nature has worked hand in hand with man to render an effect of hopeless doom. There is at this moment even thunder, crumbling with the sound of soft rock breaking, falling from a cañon wall.

Out of this place, away from implications personal to me, I escape to the band of cronies gathered about our boat below. They are Bill, the ferryman; Uncle Noey, and the Big Un.

Bill is a lank pioneer, ex-river boatman and roisterer who, weighted with growing family, has accepted this monotonous employment on the ferry.

Uncle Noey is old and short and dumpy and toothless. His lower lip protrudes. His mouth is compressed in constant grin. His eyes are merry as a puppy's. His voice remains in the register of high cackle. Uncle Noey finds every remark prostratingly funny, either as it is uttered and as all may hear, or in its potentialities which he finds secretly, with the poet's lurch to truth. So suspicious are we, in this world, of mirth that for a while I take Uncle Noey for an idiot. He, at his age, rolling in the grass,

192

coming to a stop on his belly, kicking his legs like a fawn. But he is not an idiot. He is the genius of this place; the satyr of the wood of Shiloh.

The Big Un is somewhere between six and a half and seven feet tall. "And," says Uncle Noey, "he's a runt by the side o' some we got back in the timber." Still young, he has already more paunch than symmetry will bear. His hair is blond to whiteness; eyes oyster-blue; features indistinct, taken from the mould before they have quite set. Though he is very bashful he works up courage to request "the loan" of my "spy-glass." He wishes to watch the ferry crossing the river.

"Law, hit brings 'er right up. She's a-goin' t'land right on mah shoe!"

Then, wonderingly, reversing the glass:

"Ye swap ends with hit an' hit shoves 'er a-*way* off!"

He hands me back the glasses with respectful thanks, obviously crediting me with the miracle; trying hard, though it is difficult, so big is his paw, not to touch my fingers.

The Big Un, according to the others, is a formidable fisherman. Himself, he says his luck is only "tolable." Today for instance he lost two enormous yellow cat, and a third was taken only by a thin band of lip-skin.

"Ah said t'mahysef, Ah said if he gits off Ah'm goin' t'th'ow away th'line and go in after 'im."

"Then," says Uncle Noey, "it ud'a jes ben you and him!" Uncle Noey chokes on the grass blade he has had in his teeth, wheezes and paws as if for air, transported by this vision (which through his glee becomes visible to us all) of the Big Un grappling with the cat in the foam.

Bill is telling us of a difficulty which vexed him this morning. The same drop in the water level which annoyed us left his ferryboat high and dry, tilted so that five dollars' worth of good gasoline was spilled on its deck.

Bill: "Used t'be, when we had only Wilson Dam, they give a feller warnin' an' then took three days t'let the water down. Now all to a sudden they let it down 'leven feet at a whack——"

Uncle Noey: "Not by degrees, lak the feller that et the grindstone."

Bill: "Hit makes me s'god-damned mad I'd like t'git up t'Pickwick an' tend t'that lock master m'sef. Hain't really a-goin' up thar, but if ever he comes down hyar——"

Uncle Noey: "You'll pull his tail 'til hit's plumb sore."

These men give us of the neighboring Corinth (Mississippi) police the same report as that we had of the officers of Cairo. If a man is "knowed t'be off a boat he's th'owed in jail" for the least offense. If, after the victim has sobered up, it develops that he has no money, his captain pays up in order to keep his crew together. This practice was prevalent especially in the worst years of the depression, when "taxes wuzn't a-floodin in so's to swamp nobody."

"Local boys that is knowed t'be broke," says Bill, "kin git right out in the middle of the road an' holler an' scream an' raise right smart hell. Don't nobody tetch 'em."

194

"But," adds the Big Un, "if ye've got money, ye don't have t'holler awful loud. They'd 'a th'owed me in last week if Ah hadn't run off an' left 'em."

This picture of the Big Un making off from the law, or perhaps the idea that any stub-legged officer had thought he might outrun the Big Un, is too much for Uncle Noey. He looks about as if for help, his cheeks contorted, streaming with silent tears.

But when Bill has halted too soon an account of his own last big drunk and escape from the law, now two years past, Uncle Noey finds tongue to protest: "Go on, Bill, tell the feller the whole thing; how the likker chawed yer stummick up an' ye had t'pay Doc Honeycut thirty-seven-fifty t'git hit sewed back t'gether. Law, I kin see that ole bastard squintin' his eye t'thread the needle."

The Big Un: "Man, Bill ain't a-soppin' up much these days."

Uncle Noey: "No, sir, a body kin go right up t'Bill with a bottle stickin' off his hip."

There are evidences in the park of Shiloh that the Tennessee once, instead of flowing north to Ohio, turned southward somewhere near, down toward Vicksburg and the Mississippi. There are also mounds built and left by men beyond the light not of history, but even of legend. Before the coming together of known armies here, humanity had had its time and the land was old. If there is irony now in the fact that after all that, today's incumbents are Bill and the Big Un and Uncle Noey, the

irony is faint and not disagreeable. It keeps from the foreground remembrance of other things—Albert Sidney Johnston killed and Forrest wounded; boys dead up yonder
in the hiss and spit of the Hornet's Nest; in the Peach
Orchard, with bullets clipping the blooming twigs. . . .

We leave, headed downstream toward the Ohio, making
for a camp that would be out of range of guns. Clefts
in the hills toward dark turn blue and herons cross their
blue reflection. When light is very dim white flies appear,
myriads of flies with two long threads for tails. They stay
in our hair like petals; they litter the river. Fish begin
to jump. One, then many. Their bodies bend in silver arcs
to fall. And little gothic bats come out. I dodge them
until I am tired, then sit still while they clip over. The
green-and-plum-colored mists fade out. Like a path of
ice the river keeps the light, all of the last light. In times
of deep content like this, a man is freed from all but
heartbeat, rise and fall of lung, and the roundness of
his eye.

It is late when by flashlight we land to sleep, grateful
to God among the difficult rocks.

VI

THE OHIO AND THE CUMBERLAND

# The Ohio and the Cumberland

To ENTER THE MISSOURI or the Mississippi or as now, the Ohio, from a smaller stream, is an act which custom does not dull.

Once, in a single day, I had gone from the Middle West far out on the pate of South Dakota. Overtaken by night, when dark had covered my shift from one terrain to another, I bedded down in a tourist camp. Next morning there was wind. With the same sensation as when on an ocean liner I put my shoulder to a door, and stepping over the high brass threshold, reach the deck to find the sea, I struggled to open the cabin door and stood for the first time before a true plain. I had not supposed that I could keep my feet on earth and so divine its curvature of flank, the rounding of its path in space. What I saw of earth then was a free thin line, by its unimportance dramatically important. It refused to absorb the attention, deflecting it upward into sky. A total empty cleanliness, an easement of oblivion less of earth than of something out around it. The wind, though it kept the tolling of the *Dies Iræ* and like it had tonality of hymns sung under

vaults, brought no smell of the globe; no scent whatever
of men and their enclosures, of their droppings that soil
the shoe.

So also, entering a great stream from the small, one has
an odor of the void, and sight and sound of force man
cannot quell. We who have lived through the judgment of
dust storms know that, more than plains, rivers are im-
pervious to injury from man. Forests we have done for;
coal and copper and oil we have dug and drained and
scattered; soil that was succulent humus we have bled
and left to erode, triumphing in the blight because there
was a-plenty more. But the Mississippi, the Missouri and
the Ohio, in spite of our efforts, are nearly as we found
them. They are the cream-colored mustangs that still can
beat a thunder out of earth; their nostrils swell to blood
but they will not obey.

Each time that we approach a great river, though we
know the great river now, it is with respect and fear.
For several days it is as if we sat beside high-tension wires.

This time, moving out of the vine-hung calm of the
Tennessee into the Ohio, bound for the mouth of the
Cumberland twelve miles up, we do not have time to ac-
custom ourselves to the change. After a single camp on
the north bank in Illinois, we have one morning only of
riding the Ohio. There is heat haze, and such distance to
mull over that our minds refuse. We look out at the scene
as if it were what reason would suggest, a small-scale
reproduction of itself; a museum diorama of a sector of
the globe. Contrary to its habit in August the Ohio is high

and rising higher. Opposite what we take to be the grandiose mouth of the Cumberland, it is huge.

There is no doubt of its breadth. That we can survey, crossing its every inch, swaying and foam-flecked and never arriving. But in our identification of the Cumberland we are wrong. Entering what we thought was its mouth we are overwhelmed in quick succession by the *Fairplay* of Pittsburgh, the *Jane Rhea* and the *Bob Rodes* of Louisville, the *Marcia Richardson* of Paducah—in short by so many boats that we doubt if all are descending the Cumberland from Nashville. We find that we are not only still on the Ohio, we are in its main marked channel, narrower here between island and shore—no place for us to linger in the wake of traffic.

The real embouchure of the Cumberland, when finally we discover it, astounds us. Surely we should have passed it as the entrance to a quiet creek.

We are not the first men to stand so in error. In December of 1779 there left from Fort Patrick Henry on the Holston, a fleet of settlers under John Donelson. Their plan was to enter the Tennessee, descend it (six hundred and fifty odd miles); pull up the Ohio to the Cumberland and thence to Nashborough (now Nashville), recently founded by James Robertson and an overland party.

The fleet was stopped by low water, by high water and rough water, and by "most excessive hard frost." A division of the band, sent to the rear with smallpox, was isolated by Indians and dispersed. In a narrow place between bluffs the main body was attacked, shot at from both banks. One of the boats, grounded, escaped only because its two feminine passengers, while the men fired, threw overboard baggage enough to get afloat. One of the ladies was "the night before delivered of an infant which was unfortunately killed in the hurry and confusion consequent upon such disaster." She served nonetheless, exposed to wet and cold, her clothing "very much cut with bullets."

When they reached the mouth of the Tennessee they found the Ohio swollen as we find it now. Certain of the group became discouraged, and went to Illinois; others descended the Mississippi to Natchez; Donelson and the faithful continued, requiring four days for the distance we cover in a morning, from the Tennessee to the Cumberland. Here they suffered from our present doubt. Donelson writes:

"About three o'clock, came to the mouth of a river which I thought was the Cumberland. Some of the company declared it could not be—it was so much smaller than expected. We determined, however, to make the trial, pushed up some distance and camped for the night."

And on the next day:

"We are much encouraged; the river grows wider. We are now convinced it is the Cumberland."

Nosing among the islands in the canoe, we are closer to Donelson and the colonists for Nashborough than to the citizens of modern Nashville. Here then is one condition that is not changed. This instant of losing our way, of being for a moment in a tangle of lands and waters, casts a charm before us along the whole tunnel of the Cumberland's shade. Donelson, in fact, had an advantage over us. His party and ours both reached this river without food. But whereas he may record: "We are compelled to hunt the buffalo to preserve life," my friends and I must stop to buy beef in the village of Smithland.

Smithland grew up about a plantation of the same name, property of one Colonel John Smith T. This person, to distinguish himself from other Johns of the family, and at the same time to proclaim as his place of origin the State of Tennessee, wrote after his name the initial T. He is reported to have been a gentleman of extremely courteous demeanor with, in his old age, "a venerable Daniel Boone look"; between "sudden broils" he was the mildest man that ever put bullet in a body. But he was of such temperament that his broils were as frequent as sudden, and knives and pistols, strapped to his waist and in every pocket, were almost a part of his costume. Among his slaves was one Dan, a gunsmith constantly busy in practice of his craft. The colonel lived for some time in Missouri in the early nineteenth century when the Austin family (Yankees and enemies of the colonel) were exploiting the lead mines southwest of Saint Louis. The years of Missouri's history between the colonel's arrival from Tennessee and his withdrawal after sudden broil to Kentucky are still full of echo of his doings.

## Where the Rivers Meet

The village which accumulated on his land at the mouth of the Cumberland, by contrast with his name for fire and action, is sleepy and good-natured. There is buried near by Lucy, sister of Thomas Jefferson; and the atmosphere is better suited now to tombs of ladies than to rant of broilers.

The Cumberland River in its upper reaches is an active and aerial mountain stream lovely in itself and lovely against its hills. Here at the mouth its gradient is such that when the Ohio is high—as it is now—Cumberland waters for twenty miles are held in a kind of thoughtful pool, a green and silent corridor winding, so unruffled, so richly still that up above where the water rises must be an inner home of peace.

Of men we see less than on the Tennessee (since there are no shellboats)—a few farm boys bathing, the upper half of their bodies brown except where the overall straps have crossed; a fisherman on the deck of a shanty staring, between naps, at a handful of floating jugs which, if they duck under (and if he is awake to see them), will let him know he has made a catch. And at the hamlet of Dikersville people are gathered to watch us by, summoned to the bank by our motor as by a little drum of the Cameroons.

Otherwise there are no men at all. The *Ni-sho-dse* moves evenly, effortlessly as if she took power from a third rail, secret underneath. Off the prow we see small turtles float up lazily, four legs in very ease thrust out, diving in haste before our shadow; and trim fish, long as a roasting ear, that idle to the top, round-eyed, unhurried, flashing quickly from us as if they were taken on a line suddenly taut.

These we see and nothing else, besides green plenitude of water. The Cumberland here makes a sunken road in woods, flanked by partitions of leafage "mannered" as if a gardener kept them so. We are put out of sight of all that hints of specific date within a given thousand years.

Doctor Thomas Walker, leading west his band of Virginians in 1750, discovered the mountains and the river, and named them Cumberland for William, the royal duke. If English was to be put upon the stream, Cumberland, surely, was a happy choice; unless, in a region ultimately to house so many Scots, it might be thought unkind to recall the victor of Culloden. But the good doctor, probably an incorrigibly monolingual insular, was under no necessity to devise an English name.

The stream was already called *La Rivière aux Chaouanons*, the River of the Shawanese. Most of the native names of the valley from Canada to the Gulf, from the forks of the Ohio to the Yellowstone, were gallicizations of the Indian before they were chewed still more, to fit our English mouths. Of them all surely *Chaouanon*, correctly pronounced as French, is one of the most piquant, the most titillatingly gamy and foreign. It is like that other magic French word, *les îles*, which designates collectively the Indies of the Caribbean, flushing images of colored birds and turquoise bays, amber in the shallows.

*Chaouanon* is an artist's "find"; it has on it the copper glint-among-the-leaves of North America.

The name of the tribe for itself, from which the French made *Chaouanon*, was *shawunogi*, Southerners; from *shawun*, South. In the Cumberland basin, and in an outlying colony on the Savannah in Carolina, they made up the southern advance guard of Algonquian stock. But very early in the eighteenth century they were driven out by the Chickasaws and by their former allies the Cherokees, so that only the first traders knew them on their river, and then so briefly that *Chaouanon*, the name, did not survive.*

Now, with all shut out by the steep bank and green walls, we are seeing the river probably as the *Chaouanons* saw it: or at least, say, as Andrew Jackson saw it, on his way from Nashville to Washington in 1828, moving to the White House "with the mud of all America's great rivers and swamps on his boots."

For twenty-five miles we part the silence, craning, looking in despair as night draws close, for a place to camp. Finally we spot a kind of stair made down the bank by many prints of hoofs—the lowest full of water standing in hearts, divided where mud rose up in the groove of the toe. In the days of Robertson and Sevier and Boone,

---

*Except for this, that after the French, early river travellers called the ridges and bluffs along the Mississippi, from Cape Girardeau to Saint Louis, the *Oshawanos*—reducing to one noun a part of the phrase [*Montagnes*] *aux Chaouanons*, as from *aux Ark*[*ansas*] they made *Ozark* and from *aux Kas*[*kaskias*], *Okaw*. The Mississippi hills about Cape Girardeau were so called because the Shawanese, from 1793, were encouraged to settle there by the governor, Baron de Carondelet.

of Herrod and Kenton, these would mark a water hole for buffalo. Donelson here might stop his boats and station hunters. To us it means domestic cows, maybe a clearing on the bank, and a farm near by with milk and food.

Sure enough there is at the top of the stair a flat place, dark under limbs that flatten out over our heads. Beyond is a hay field still in sun, still warm to our feet, recently cut and headily aromatic. Beyond again is a white farmhouse with large and excellent chimney. Evidently there are, inside, fireplaces velvet with soot, violet with ash, open, not yet dishonored. From the yard of this house there is view on the Cumberland in a good bend, and over cornfields, tasselled precisely in detail, yet in the whole, confused like the heads of crowds. There are grazing lands, there are fat cattle, and there are fine folk to match these things.

Two little boys who have climbed a tree giggle because at first I cannot find them. They talk to me freely beginning or ending every sentence with *sir*. Their shepherd dog thrusts his nose to my palm, pushing gently upward. A woman appears on the gallery to see what we want. Her hair is combed straight back so that its neatness is its only art. Her house dress is clean. Her bare arms, bare legs, bare feet are clean. Her face glows with hospitality and soap. She has an air that makes us know she spends her life in service of others. But with her it is not useless abnegation, nor self-conscious, nor suppliant of help. Like great physical beauty it is in itself a career, self-supporting within its borders. But she cautiously declines to allow us to camp, or promise sale of chickens, without the word of her man. He will be in soon from the fields. A girl is calling him now, pulling and releasing the rope of a bell whose echo is polished with tolling of years on the same rock. Unless we are sent a messenger in a few minutes we shall know that we have permission to camp and that, in the morning, the man will bring us chickens.

Under the leaves on the flat we set the tent and make our fire and sleep. In the dark there roams the smell of cedar smoke, of humus and wet leaves and dung of cows. The cattle stand here in the shade of afternoon; about us, so that we have to walk with care, are many "patties" round and sunk in the center. Here in the open air, over the scent of earth and hay, the smell of dung is a good smell. Its integrity is square-set.

Before we are up in the morning we hear the steps of a man; and a voice, cheerful with summer dawn, rings out:

"Hey, you fellers! Hello-o-oh! Hey! I've carried down them roosters you fellers wanted."

We tumble out one after another, having each put on, out of respect for a man of Kentucky, a pair of jockey-shorts. He exclaims, as if he were tapping a bird-box to make the wrens fly out:

"Well, I'll be God damned! They's *three* of ye! And you 'ith nothin' on but them little pants. Lucky thing I didn't send down one o'th'gals."

The roosters are young and tender. They are already picked, cut up and salted, floating in a pan of water they have made pinkish with their blood. There are four, and unless it is too much (he doesn't want to rob anybody) the man asks a dollar.

But he is less interested in this transaction than in the *Ni-sho-dse*, tethered below in the willows.

"Man!" he says. "Man alive! I'd miss a crop if I had that!"

It has been his life's wish to get in a boat and start somewheres. He'd do it tomorrow if it weren't for his wife.

"Women—they hep ye in a way. But sometimes they ain't nothin' so laborious fer a man as t'be hepped by a lady."

Every man in this whole region of the rivers, even those engaged in formal river traffic, is possessed of the same desire; just to get in a small boat and go. It has been so since men have known these streams; since the days when the Cumberland, the Ohio and the Mississippi were called the "three rivers," meaning three that made one road to Saint Louis and New Orleans. The reader of any biography of a man of this country will find, in the first chapter, that when he was a boy he made a raft and went down the Cumberland or the Tennessee. So young Sam Houston. So even Thomas Jonathan Jackson, already solemn, already *fato profugus*. In this travel of our own I give way to the same urge, but, in time and geography, I am reversing directions. I am working back home. Followed to its head the path would lead to Ulster and to Scotland.

Beyond this camp the river becomes a little clearer and

swifter. It winds, it winds, it winds, between banks impenetrable except to axemen. We see nothing and hear nothing but water until we reach the village of Kuttawa; then Eddyville, where there is a prison of "Gothic" architecture, so that one might mistake it for a church or college. Most of the men confined within are probably farm and hill-country boys. Is it an added punishment that they are kept in sight of woods where they may number ducks in flight, where but for a width of wall freedom would be so sweet?

There is also at Eddyville, and immediately below the prison, a dam. For a distance above it, naturally, the water is pooled. Now, with the water so high, it moves over the concrete line in a fold, steady. Like so much glass it betrays no force or motion. But when it has reached the level below-dam, it throws up a foam like the mane of a circus horse and as gay; whipping back on the calm fold that looks still, it is turned under with a crackle as of sparks. Beyond this point the surface of the river is smooth a brief way, boiling then wildly, to settle in muscles and buttocks of overlapped force too hard, too strong for foam or noise.

Below the lock we halloo for admission. Our voices are shattered and carried up into all Eddyville by the gate. But no one comes. Seeing, at the far end of the grounds pertaining to the dam, two men cutting grass, I go to them asking where the lock master may be found. They look at one another with the neck motion of two geese. They put down their scythes, running their palms along the leg seams of their overalls. They sit down heavily in the grass. One of them, pulling a seeded stem to hold in his teeth, looks off with the air of a man determined not to commit himself. The other asks: "Ye want t'get through the lock?"

I might have answered: "No, I just like to see gates opened. I am a taxpayer. Let me see you work." But somehow I scent behind their affected stupidity the hilarity, much compressed, of a rural joke. Therefore, when one points up to the prison, saying: "Mister, ye'll have t'go up yonder t'git permission," I am prepared for him.

"Oh, then you are convicts! Excuse me, I'll just step up and speak with your guard."

There is an instance of silence. The man who spoke looks up with the gaze of a pig shot between the eyes with a twenty-two. He of the seeded stem rolls in the grass:

"That's one ye kain't chalk up, Ben! That's one ye didn't make! Ben, y'ain't fooled noboddy this time!"

When the last ripple of this titanic joke has spread its force, my comedians confess that they are indeed in charge of the lock and that they will let us through.

"Couldn't keep ye out, mister," says Ben, pulling at the hairs of his nose and examining his finger. "All you'd have t'do 'ud be t'write a letter t'th'gov'mint."

When they have "rested" and "gone to get a drink," we start for the lock. But even then there is delay. Ben halts in the path and turns back:

"Mister, ye'll have to 'scuse me a minute. My old kidneys is hangin' over my belt like a pair o' saddle bags."

# Where the Rivers Meet

We find a night's camp on a bank so high that only the minimum baggage is got up. A man slinks from the woods, descending, with no greeting, to a boat hidden below, making off with oarlocks that give out the sound of a crutch on wooden stairs. Thirty ducks go by in one band, and a heron, clipping willows, passes level with our heads. Then it is dark, and there are, by exception, no mosquitoes. We lie in the open counting falling stars, listening to owls, our cheeks nudged by fireflies. In the dead of night comes a fog that condenses, running down the indented center of every leaf, dropping on the tent as on a loose drum.

This morning we delve on through woods to Rockcastle—so named on the map but barely a hamlet. Far above our heads on a bluff by the landing are painted the flood marks since the '80's. They are eloquent to one who knows the meaning of *high water;* eloquent much more yet for one remembering how the river made the bluff, before the *Chaouanons* and buffalo, before the French and Spanish and the Ulster Scots. No wonder its eye looks old and has such light.

At the top of the ferry road one store is in sight. It has the sign: *Cold Beer.* But the kindly proprietress explains that she has long since ceased to handle beer. The sign was put there long ago. It has just never been taken down. Nothing in the country is ever taken down. Things moulder and fall. They are grown over and eaten away. It is that way in the country. In old barn lofts a little hay is left, blackened, covered with web, seeds in it

sprouted by rain that drips through the roof. In abandoned well houses a melon seed, dropped between the
floor-boards, sends up a runner; at midsummer in the
sonorous shade will lie a melon, runty and pale, the
pattern of its markings like a snake's. On hay and vine
the light will fall through cracks, active with motes,
crossed by buzzing flies, silent until some one comes. All
this is a part of the charm of the country.

Turning from the store, facing away from the river,
I am surprised by the sight of all we miss below on the
water. The country off east is made up entirely of hills
crumpled like a rug, like the lower Appalachians which
Indians called the *Endless Mountains:* range after range
forested, blue blue-green, sunlit and pocked with shadow
of cloud. Below me, facing so, there is a house where I
should gladly stop. It is T-shaped, with the head of the
letter fronting the road. It is of board now unpainted,
but its lines are so reasonable and so restrained; its chimneys are of such tasteful work; its vines and junipers, its
fence and mailbox, its quiet smoke so humbly good, that
one's heart turns over. If we had not accustomed our
bellies to diet of husk instead of corn (as to drugs that
violently keep alive a while before they kill) we should
each have a home like this. When I have "earned what
I have inherited from my fathers, and so possess it";
when I am worthy, I hope I may come to a place like
this, and make my life a well-eye.

Toward Canton we are threatened by rain. In the deep

groove of the river thunder rolls. If there is light above
we cannot see it here, as in steep valleys day is quick to
leave and slow to come. The water turns black and reflects exceptionally, like cypress swamps in the Charleston
gardens, mirroring azaleas in their ink.

Canton appears on its hills, seen through trees as all
is, here; a cluster of houses about a church that lost its
spire. The one street is an old state road for the carting
of freight from the landing. Canton then served as *dépôt*
for the country, and Canton now has the look of a place
until lately covered by water or ash, on which the light
now falls—history or the milieu of history made visible,
but not quite as it was; lacking the glow of blood beneath
the skin; wistful, musty with regret. There is a galleried
brick tavern, with handsome lines and three-foot walls,
built to be a joyous place. There are houses with chimneys of good character, suggesting the hearths inside. And
there is the doleful church, near collapse, but once a monument of some charm. Life has gone around Canton, sap-
ping its strength. "A fine ole place forty year ago. These
days there ain't no money and nothin' doin'. Folks is jest
too po', jest too po'."

Laden with water jugs, we are only halfway down to
the boat when the rain breaks, showing pearl in clefts of
rock and woods. Hills and the bridge of Canton then are
blotted out. The world for us shrinks to a field of corn
below, nervous, disturbed as a herd is disturbed. The boat,
when we reach it, is full to the brim. We stand in the
soft mud, ankle deep in the shallows, bailing water enough

to find a place to sit. We work slowly. Once more there is no reason to hurry out of rain.

Around a bend we come upon the steamer *Tennessee* and the dredge-boat *Kentucky,* both, for our good luck, stationary. And we pass a second dam, luring the attendants, as at the first, from tasks unrelated to the opening of locks. Here the grounds and buildings stand in the foreground of no village. They lie on a slope alone, on a lawn encircled by woods that are old and dark and dripping. Below them the river is profound and jet, burnished, its lamina of reflection foreshortening such distance of air above that the depth of water beneath is one's second thought. Moving so fast that it is not seen to move, the flank of water over the dam ends its fall in a selvage of foam curiously particular, curiously active, standing against the wet agate of the woods as in an interval of the stereoscope, artfully false.

Because this scene is so well groomed, the country beyond seems forbidding. Then it rains. Looking up we can follow the lines of it, each with length and elevation, like a full vein. For a while it stops. The air is filled with globules we cannot see except where they collect in pockets as mist, or separately fall on cloth. The water standing on leaves drips occasionally, heavy, making a splash like heron droppings, except that it is not white and does not leave the oily circle. Then rain breaks again.

The river is rising and rising alarmingly. It would be well to get a camp to serve for several days. At least, by lying against one another in the tent, we could get warm. But there is nowhere to land. The banks are steep and muddy. They are endless. There is no parenthesis in the woods.

At last, near a village at the south line of Kentucky (its name is my secret) we find a high plateau spread between two slopes. To reach it in the mud we are forced to make a path that turns and parallels itself before it turns again, as in mountains one lets a horse up or down an incline. Once arrived at the top it is not bad. It would be splendid if it were not wet. Surrounded on two sides and at the back by rising ground, our site is flat, wooded with oak and silver shag-bark. Branches intermingle above with the ramifications of banyan trees; outward from camp, over the gummy slide to the Cumberland, they grow long and straight, being in that direction unimpeded. Between their final tips and the bank is left a space, a transom down which we look at the river.

Two days later we are still in this place. In one night the river has come up twelve feet. It is angry and covered with driftwood. There is no reason to risk ourselves upon it, even if we dared. Walking along a path grown with briars and deep cane below the bluffs, we can reach the village and get a little canned goods. There is not anything else to buy. It does not matter. We cannot make a fire to cook. On the first morning, with gasoline from the fuel can, we produced a smudge to heat water for coffee. On the second we failed. The rain put it out.

All our clothing is wet and muddy. Since it does not

keep us warm we have taken it off. We are curled like unfeathered nestlings, trying to find how this situation may be made agreeable. We have one book, a Bible in French, from which we read aloud. Now and then a man gets up to leave, walking naked in the rainy woods. He has what is called in the West, "cabin fever." He has to get out.

As the same weather continues, the four corners of the tent soak through. Then the lower slopes of the walls spring leaks. Baggage, beds and men are piled center about the pole. And the reading goes on:

*"De même aussi un lévite, arrivé dans cet endroit, il est venu, et en le voyant, il a passé outre. Mais un Samaritain, qui voyageait. . . ."*

The charmed balance of this, heard over the drum of rain and the rising Cumberland, sets up an interest on which for a time we can feed. In me, at least, there is a numbed atavism stirring its feelers. My ancestors, too, stopped by wilderness streams to read in that book. And if I hear it differently, I find the same calm, and wear it as an amulet.

But in the night comes a rain eclipsing others. The last dry spot in the world—the peak of our roof—gives way, sending down streams. Unable to sleep we lie on the baggage, each man with the head of another in his lap, lighting one cigarette from another. In the glare of the match, water on the floor, collected in pools, rolls as if it had the consistency of blood.

This cannot last. Therefore in council we examine plans.

217

A cave is near at hand. We might go into it. But its narrow mouth slopes down, stony and slick, to the first chamber in which we might stand. There would be dark and glacial cold. Rather we shall abandon the tent where it is, walk to the village, and ask permission to sleep in a barn. If we are refused we shall risk the boat in the river, descend to Eddyville, and accept the humiliation of a good warm inn.

This morning, leaving the tent to execute these plans, I catch sight of something out of the corner of my eye. A tall old man stands watching me under the trees. He has already decided that I am harmless. He says:

"Howdy, son."

He has not, as in other regions well he might, come to drive us from his land. He defines the limits of his property, placing it all at our disposal:

"Anyway, it's gov'mint land t'th' top o' the bank. I couldn't git shet of ye if I wanted to."

Also he says:

"You ain't no revenooers. Y'ain't the kind that'ud be selling Bibles."

These being so many affirmations, and true, I let them stand.

"Air ye bug hunters?"

"No, sir."

"Geologists?"

"No, sir."

"Then they ain't nothin' left but jest t'be out a-seein'

the country. Reminds me o' days when I's a loggin'."

After a pause he adds:

"Hit's a-rainin'."

Then:

"Hit's *ben* a-rainin' for the least while back."

Then:

"Boy, you look like you'd ben rolled in ——."

Finally, as if compelled to it by his heart, after manful resistance to the temptation to meddle in another's business, he says what is on his mind:

"Whyn't y'all come home with me?"

And, on the defensive, excusing this intrusion:

"Y'ain't used t'livin' out. Y'all goin' t'be sick."

I point out that his wife might not be pleased to receive three bums who seem to be rolled in ——.

"If Mom knowed you's out hyar, sh'd git you in if she had t'switch yore laigs the whole way home."

But has he room in his house?

"Ain't aimin' t'take ye t'my house. I'm aimin' t'give ye a whole house. Got two."

Picking up our kitchen equipment and our bedding, we start up the hill after Uncle Rob. That is the name he says we are to give him. Up and up and up, into a hill finely wooded with oak and walnut, hickory and Osage orange, and mottled beech with ebony-stem ferns between their toes.

Uncle Rob is somewhat rheumatic. He climbs slowly and with constraint, as if he had an egg in his pocket. Frequently he pulls up to a halt, slapping familiarly, as one feels a horse's buttock, one of his trees:

"Now this hyar's a chestnut. Don't see many chestnuts these days, an' these hyar ain't none too peart."

When we have got high enough to see over the country he pulls us by the sleeve, pointing to a thread of blue cabin smoke rising from the woods:

"Henry McNamorra lives thar."

Or he singles out an island where he used to make a crop of corn when he was younger, naming the bushels he got to an acre. The soil, he says, is as rich "as a foot up a bull's ass."

To all this we answer: "Yes, sir," but we do not follow very well because we are dazed by Uncle Rob's hospitality. It has something gallantly, something fantastically incongruous; as if, through air tumbling with fat snow, he had brought an armload of sweet peas.

The house to which he leads us is on the crest we have been climbing. The hill is sharply rounded here so that straight ahead there is view over the ranges of Kentucky into Tennessee; and below, as down the side of an egg, there is Uncle Rob's village. It is a group of cottages with long roofs and deep galleries. Each seems to have turned upon itself like a hound to lie down under its trees and flowers. Only a few of the newer ones seem to have been built there. The rest are ancient and settled, and seem to have been occupied by man for a long time, but in the origin accidentally, as birds appropriate a natural shelter. To the right of the village, folds of the hills emit the Cumberland. To the left mounts a yellow road. Model-T's come down it bobbing; a rider makes from the woods, his mare attacking the mud with elegant concern.

The house is one in which, years ago, Uncle Rob and his ole woman began their life together. It is a two-room cabin, with uncertain additions tacked on behind. Each room has a fireplace with whitewashed brick front, with sunken rock hearth. The walls have been papered many times (each has left its record) and once with newspapers. I am able, so, to review the events of the Harding administration, and the jubilee of the Nizam of Hyderabad. The place has been uninhabitated so long that it has no human smells. There are mice and roaches and spiders and dust. A cake of wet soot breaks from the chimney and falls, scattering black beads that have a point of blue. All this we note, but not to blame. Grateful for roof and fire we sit turning the steaming bed clothes, wishing that we might remain all summer, all fall, until winter when the odd-shaped panes would have a plush of hoar.

Failing this we stay at least several days. Our limbs relax in warmth. Our spirits rise. We miss none of the delight of owning peaks of Kentucky with a view over Tennessee. By day vague clouds come trailing by, blotting from sight the violet pockets of the hills, familiar, domestic as the mouse-nosed mules that snort and stamp in the yard. At night the stars are nearer about us, immediate as fireflies at our knees in stems of oats, curious, persistent, like the eyes of young opossums, of many little foxes in the black.

## Where the Rivers Meet

We have numerous visits from Uncle Rob. He wakes us early, sure that any sleeper after dawn will be glad to be roused, though of course he will be a little sheepish about it.

"Well, damn *me!*" Uncle Rob says, sticking his head through the window. "Sun up fer an hour an' you fellers still sawin' gourds! Law, this puts me in mind o'th' days when I was raftin' logs. A ole empty house an' eight 'r ten of us layin' around. Fellow's a fool not to know when he's lucky, but whenever I see a raft goin' by hit nearly kills me b'cause I ain't on it."

Then he settles for long talks. Uncle Rob is a militant agrarian. He is God damned sick of seeing all our little money going North for machinery; for machinery that wouldn't be needed if folks had any sense; for machinery whose payments and upkeep enslave the "possessor," so that he becomes like an artilleryman attached to a field-piece and no farmer at all. The happy man and the sage is one with few acres. He has a team of mules and a good brood sow which produce their kind, making natural replacements, needing no gas or oil. He goes out in winter to "fork down" a little fodder for his cattle in the snow: he hauls their manure out to spread on his "pore spots." He keeps away from cities and he keeps his chillern out of cities. Folks that in the country are up-standing white folks "turns t'pure trash in town."

"Damn the fine roads," shouts Uncle Rob. "Plough 'em up an' let a part o' the country go back to game. Steamboats is good enough t'ship on. *Shore* they take longer!

That's jest what I'm a-tellin' ye. With trucks an' them roads a man gits his money too fast an' too often an' he spends it the same way. Things *ought* t'take longer. They ain't s'much to life but what ye kin live it up before yore time an' then set a-starin' like a pore dumb fool—or worse, gittin' int'trouble b'cause ye've got time on yore hands. Take that young buck that come back from town th'other night drunk, drivin' fast and shootin' wild fer pure fun. Shot a girl a-settin' on her own gallery. Shore hit was an accident. He didn't have nothin' agin her—jest made a mis-lick an' hit her. What right's *he* got to a autymobile? Them cars is jest like jobs in town an' all th'rest. They give a feller that ain't got no guts a-tall the idea that he's *somethin'*. He can let on like he's a real man."

"Shore I know ye think like I do," Uncle Rob concedes, mollified by my truthful protest, but keeping his head up, as if it had on it a bonnet of dyed feathers. "I knowed ye would th'day ye named them ferns I couldn't name m'sef."

Down in the village Uncle Rob is a sort of squire. His word counts. He tells us that he has cleared things up so's folks is goin' t'be friendly right off. Things needed clearing because, while we were camped below, folks had heard our motor approach and stop and not go on. Boys had been dispatched to find what was what. Covertly from the brush they had inspected us. We were plainly "revs." If we weren't a pack of egg-sucking weasels we'd have run up the Federal flag and got it over with. Now they knew that the Bible salesman who had passed through a

223

fortnight before was not a Bible salesman after all. He was a "spotter" masked in Holy Writ. We were the "follow up men." Our continued silence in one place had had a particularly depressing effect upon everybody. It was thought especially disloyal. Folks were restless. Our every movement was known, discussed, weighed and judged by the men about the store.

Now appears Uncle Rob in their midst, shaking his cane under their noses, denouncing their treatment of honest boys. Each man assures me privily then, that he knew me to be no "rev" the whole while, and he reckons he doesn't know my name. Some are not satisfied with name; they wish to know my names, not first, middle and last, but the names of families to which I am related. Nor or they content to hear that I am from Missouri.

"Folks *has*," one man suggests, "gone to Missouri from other places."

He nods as I say that my people were from Alabama and Tennessee. Later he introduces me to his wife, proudly as if I had composed a scherzo or improved a toothpaste tube.

"His folks wuz born and bred in Tennessee," adding, to head off her question, "Allisons, Richardsons, Shelleys, Wards, Roberts."

"Law," the woman exclaims, "we've knowed all *them* folks!"

And she looks at me intently, as if at a returned cousin, seeking in the adult face lineaments of a youth she had known when she was a girl.

# The Ohio and the Cumberland

There comes a day when there is no rain, but only threat of rain, so that we gather courage to go on our way. As my friends return to the original camp to bring the boat to the village landing, I go down the hill to say good-by to Uncle Rob.

I find an automobile of gay color at the door. Smokey Cal, a git-tarist, and his assistant, a fiddler, are in from Texas, selling patent medicines. On the gallery and in the yard forty or fifty men are gathered.

Those sitting near Uncle Rob lean over to whisper in his ear news of my arrival. They make no effort to welcome me. It is not only that they are for the moment guests at Uncle Rob's house; Uncle Rob, anywhere, is the man who "takes holt." Now he descends the steps, takes me by the elbow, parting the way to a seat on the porch. The crowd looks up as at a hanging. "Boys," says Uncle Rob to Smokey Cal and his podner, "I want you t'meet my friend. Ye can tell by the way his eyes is sot in his skull an' the way his nose is stuck of his face, he ain't no Yankee. Shake the hand of a man that's come back home. He's with us, boys. You play him a perty tune."

Smokey Cal handles the git-tar, and he is the one of the two who sings. He has sparse gray hair, pop-eyes, and a hollow convict cheek. His fiddler is young. He has a well-shaped body, a sensual mouth, a roving glance. A ripple runs over him as he plays, as if in excitement under caress. The young women stare at him.

The two break into a wailing song in which there is question of a man gwine down to the rivah (gwine take his rockin' chair). This kind of stuff is perhaps not music, or exists only in the margin of music, remotely akin. But well done in its native setting it has unholy charm. The loping, loose-shouldered notes of the git-tar, the fiddle, the voice black-edged with grief, have between them the "lone" of mountain horizons and the palor of unfriendly moons. Hearing, you know why the hound throws back his ears at night, and why he bays.

> "Whiskey's gwine drive me crazy.
> Cocaine gwine kill mah baby.
> Pretty girls gwine cause me t'loose mah mind!
> Ah got drunk on o-o-old Mau-u-ud
> Oh Lawd! Oh Lawd!
> Ain nobody's business but mi-i-i-ne!"

Enchanted, the men in the yard look up, open-mouthed, forgetful of self as when they watch a circus clown or an organ-grinder's monkey. The boy who sits on the step is dumb and stares, but I doubt if he sees. Visibly he is alone, but a golden-haired girl has her head in his lap, I am sure. She is reaching up her arms to pull him down. The vision is opposed by all without; but it is in him safely, as in a watch one wheel is nestled within another, two moving in contrary directions.

At the far end of the gallery sit Uncle Rob's niggers, on the floor.

"Them's my boys," he explains.

And they call out as if answering the roll:

"Yas*suh*, Mist' Rob!"

226

"At's right, Mist' Rob!"

"They's good boys. Goin' t'cut wood a heap better after this music."

More than the whites, they are transported. As in moments of fleshly love their skin and eye are bright. They crouch, rubbing their wool with the full palm of the hand, twitching, rolling their eyes, adding to the song, skillfully timed in an interval, a rich: "Bawm . . . bawm . . . bawm!"

Seeing stragglers at the edge of the crowd throw up their heads to listen and then move away (vexed that everything should happen on the same morning), I know they have heard my motor. Shaking hands with Uncle Rob, I go into the house to find his wife, with whom are gathered modestly, away from the men, the women listeners. I offer her payment for the cabin we have had.

"Rob," she says, " 'ud run me off the place. Besides, it ain't what we're told. It ain't no way t'take in the stranger within yore gates."

Some of the men have got to the landing when I arrive. Others, along the way, I see start, reaching for their hat and walking stick. This is the way things enter their lives. They hear them and go look. Then they turn the impression over in their minds. Whatever enters else comes in as legend, as the long-protracted shadow of the thing itself.

At the last moment Uncle Rob appears at the water's edge. He has remembered that he had a present for me.

Into my hand he presses something round and cold and hard.

"Ye needn't look at it now. It's a piece of grapeshot I got out of a tree at Donelson. Mills down at Padooky won't take any timber from up thar. Tears up their saw-bands."

The river we face is far from encouraging. It has risen over twenty feet since the day we saw it first. It is yellow and swift. The quiet sections where we might have greater ease are literally paved with driftwood. Old logs lie half submerged; whole trees float by, leaf and branch, trunk and root. Keeping close to shore, following indentations of the willows, frightening ducks, moving through water still stirred by their rising, we make it as far as Fort Donelson, Dover, and a little above.

But there, having no desire to see how long a canoe can drive against logs without breaking up, we turn and quit the Cumberland. In a single day and a half, with motor and current, we reach the Ohio. The way is difficult, requiring constant vigilance. There is driftwood not only in sight, but hidden. And we pass steamers—the *Wyconda* and the *J. Z. W.*, monstrous, hissing through the woods. Their pilots lean from the wheel, flexing a brown goose-egg of upper arm in greeting. But this time we cannot answer. Their wake is pounding us with blows that might also be inflicted by swinging at us a half dozen bricks in a gunnysack.

There are moments to redeem all this. The river is flowing now full from willow to willow, with no muddy shore line. Placed up so high we can see about us, as we could not on the upstream trip, into panoramas of wet woods, glittering so that they seem to be coated with thin ice. In the dark of rain to come and hush of rain just past, the air seems another element, manifest more solidly, like glass or water that, if it were not tinted green, would be invisible. Landing on honest soil to lunch, we look as out of divers' helmets. Familiar leaves are "set" with the precision of sponge and coral in a depth.

At the end of the first day we find camp at the edge of a new-cut hay field, under elms, where the mower has turned aside, leaving a diamond shape untouched. There is a half moon whose light gives the field the look of snow, stained by the shadows of tent and trees.

The morning of the second day is gloomy. Wanly at intervals the sun appears, barely allowing time for clouds to reflect in water. When at noon we pull in once more to Smithland, there is driving rain. It lets up enough that as we leave we can note the sudden distance of perspective into the Ohio, through and over the collection of islands at the mouth of the Cumberland.

Nearly all islands in the Missouri, the Mississippi, and the Ohio have this in common; they are wooded so thickly that foliage rises and leans out from them, like plumes from the corners of a royal coach or as in an emblem of heraldry. For their height the water seems the flatter. And the water eats into them, under their penchant limbs, so that they stand out against it with neatness rare except where air is thin and land is stark. To be sure, if

229

you land in the islands, this impression of scissor sharpness is not borne out. Islands in these rivers are in process of formation and decay, as in space stars assembled from primeval matter are strewn at some interval of development from glowing cloud to spirals. The crust of young islands will not hold you up. The old are dotted with swamps. And both are rank with vegetation that will sting your face and cling to your ankles and make you sweat.

But from a boat, from a canoe with paddle uplifted, in the rain, with thrushes singing out of them (intense as some vast instrument momentarily muted) the islands one and all seem lands exempt, orderly as one first saw them. Now as we leave the Cumberland, one of them ahead catches sun, doubly then an island in the drizzle; as in the West, after a night that was like to have no dawn, one peak of several is first to find light.

Lifting Cumberland webs from our hair, squaring our shoulders, we are sucked out, for the last time, where banks are far apart. On the Ohio a cold wind blows. It moves upstream, raising such a sea that it would ground us if we were not moving with it. We pitch and jab the prow and coast unevenly, our whole length sometimes button-holed with foam. Out of a straight line with the wind, in a crossing, we are roughly handled. Surrounding us are water-forms that would be cones except that their tips are cut, throwing spray that is white as smoke before the burst of flame.

## The Ohio and the Cumberland

In Kentucky range after range of hills come up on a southwest bias, some of them touched with light and bodiless with it. Below Galconda, Illinois breaks into fine palisades. Galconda itself (or what we see of it) is an unsightly town. Except for a monument on the courthouse lawn, it has no memory of the days when it was Sarahville, founded by the widow Sarah Lusk, who, with a son, a slave, and a rifle, ran the ferry.

But the town is redeemed by its natural setting. Opposite and a little above, crossing the pitch of the river, in haze of Confederate gray lit with sunset, we camp in an island bay which does not face the water in its breadth, but which is turned so that the view is downstream. We fling ourselves without speaking on the first dry bank we have seen in days. There are terraces of sand, white as that one buys from the florist to plant winter narcissus; it is warm between our toes. Stripping, we soap our bodies slowly, with the care and knit brow of raccoons that dip their food, even though it dissolve, into water. It is a great boon to the spirit that we need no longer be filthy, that we need not smell like wet dogs.

Out of the colored haze comes a boat, and out of the boat a man who rents this island, remaining on it five days a week during summer, to make a crop of corn. He is large and rotund and jolly. His eye is blue, with very black lash. When we ask if he lives in Illinois he says, Hell, no, can't we see he is a Kentuckian? He maintains that at county fairs on the Illinois side any one, with ordinary eyesight and a modicum of natural decency, can pick out the Kentuckians.

231

He urges us to come inland to his shack to have a dinner of sowbelly and corn, and to stay all summer. "Kentuckians," he says solemnly, "and Missourians, has always ben brothers." When we counter with an invitation to eat with us, he accepts. He is interested in the steak we have bought in Galconda. To him it is "winter meat," now piquantly out of season. But he is not content without bringing a share. He disappears into the field, emerging with ears of corn laid along his arm, like stove wood.

"Anybody else 'ud a-ben into that already," he says. "Them bastards on the shanty boats 'ud already had it shucked an' ben out lookin' fer a hawg t'shoot."

As he sits chewing the tough meat he tells us about himself. He is a Southerner "born and bred." "This government" still owes his family for thirty-six hundred dollars' worth of horses collected for Forrest, but stolen by Federal troops. However, he is not an uncritical admirer of his country. He has seen farmers farther south, for instance, planting nothing but cotton, and he thinks they are a pack of lunk-heads. In what way are they more independent than wage-earners in industry, he wants to know—and they "liable t'be with nothin' to put in their mouths, a-standin' right thar on their own land!"

He himself has been tempted by no such folly. He plants and raises such variety of things that neither market nor drought nor untimely frost can send him, quite, to the dole. "I ain't never got none o' that P. W. A. money," he says. "I ain't never had time." What, he demands to be told, do we think he has had to buy at the grocery, and in eighteen years of married life? Nothing but salt, sugar, coffee and "sody." Nothing else. Not even soap. From his own land he has corn, wheat, tobacco, poultry, eggs, fruit, vegetables, peanuts and popcorn. His wife makes her own bread. She cans even frying-size chickens for winter. He keeps young Jerseys bred so's t'have three-four always fresh. He sees to it that there are hams in the smoke house, and quarters of veal, hung until they have a thin crust.

"That-a-way," he concludes, "they kain't nothin' tetch me."

He is puzzled to know what he would do in a city. He couldn't sleep much after three-thirty, he is sure. "An' I know I'd never git used t'not goin' out t'th'barn t'feed a few little pigs."

In the morning we set out, excited as by a start from scratch, in sun and wind and fast-moving cloud. Crossing the wake of the *Pioneer*, we land in Illinois at the town of Rosiclare. Here it is my turn to guard boat, and while my friends are shopping in the stores, I am entertained by the mistress of a shanty.

She ushers me aboard protesting that she ain't had time to give the place a lick this morning, that, inside, it going to look like "the hind wheel of destruction." She wears, evidently, nothing but her house dress, since through a tear her navel shows like an archer's target. Her heels are high and much run over. Her nails are scarlet.

In the big room which is the whole interior of the boat, she calls my attention to a wedding license, recently framed, which she thinks is "right perty." It is dated not long back, though the room is milling with chillern. The youngest, a girl just able to hold up her head, is lying on the bed in the middle of a wet spot, cooing and reaching for her feet. Her nails are also scarlet.

My hostess is mistress of the leafy parenthesis. She says:

"Well, I tell you when I seen Joe a-tuggin' on that net thinkin' hit wuz full o' fish, an' me knowin' all the time hit wuz stuck on a log (him a-pullin' an' a-strainin' till ye could 'a knocked his eyes off with a stick! Law, I reckon ye know who mends nets around hyar when they git busted! Zeke, honey, jest clear off that cheer an' set thar out o' the gentleman's road!) I jest couldn't hep it —I layed right back and hollered."

She is somewhat hard to follow. You must pay close heed, as to a parlor magician with cards. Yet such style is not without advantage. A period brings with it a flush of arrival; one has got home; one may take off one's hat and fan.

We pass Elizabethtown without stopping, noting, however, at the landing, the showboat *Majestic* and her tug, rewarded for inferior size by the name *Attaboy*. The people below this point have been telling us about the *Majestic*, as on other streams they have spoken of other showboats. Evidently, like the American Indian, the packet and the saddle horse, the showboat has simply "layed low" during a period of supposed eclipse.

234

## The Ohio and the Cumberland

We halt at the village of Cave-in-Rock (a short distance downstream from the cave itself), naïvely disappointed to find in this quiet hamlet of sun and bees and hollyhocks no outward sign of the depravity which shanty folk the length of the Ohio have insisted is its chief characteristic. "Cave-in-Rock," our friend Rafe had said, "is *bad*, and it's *ben* bad sense the beginnin' o' time." In territorial days already this region was infested with river pirates—notably those who made their headquarters in the cave near by; rascals of the same stamp as the "land pirates" who lay in the woods on trails leading north from New Orleans, and the criminals of river dives in Natchez and Memphis. When Illinois was a young state too large to govern well, this element of the population formed in gangs and clans, sometimes taking matters into their own hands. If the shanty men are well informed, the country was never completely freed of the scourge. When seeds of the evil days of Prohibition came they fell here on a culture bed, in a land well trained for violence.

The Cave-in-Rock from which the village takes its name is easily reached from the river. If it were not for the legend, for the tale of a hidden chimney leading to chambers full of skeletons, sprawled and merry of grin by lantern light, no one would stop. As caves go this one is commonplace—a simple opening in the shape of an oval lying on its side, eighty feet across and two hundred deep, with nothing to command attention but its cool. Undoubtedly across this clammy room men were kicked and dragged, bleeding and with bones already broken, up to their death. Undoubtedly they screamed and the hollow rock received the scream with care. But all today is still. From forty-eight states and Hawaii tourists have come to scratch their names on the wall. Facing outward the dark is slit with the oval of light. Between the fawn and white sycamore trunks the Ohio flows. Over it, piled from the level dew-point, are clouds becalmed above the wind of earth.

Beyond Caseyville we make a camp on the Illinois side, below a cliff. Two boulders, forty feet high, have fallen here, leaving between themselves and the cliff and between one another, dark avenues. These rocks, squared as if for fortress walls, have lain here long, worn by the currents during floods. Their surfaces "flow" as if laid on with a knife; they are pocked where the active water has found a feeble spot and eaten in. On the inside of the avenues they make, in constant shade, they are covered with a velvet of short bright moss and a longer dark-green moss like the tips of juniper branches, growing in and around the nostrils of the water pits.

Here where trees and rocks and moss are mottled with sun, alive with shadows that move in and out of place, we pitch the tent. It is little, but swollen, sonorous as a fiddle in wind that sucks between the stones.

At night, simultaneously with the moon and obscuring the moon, comes a gale out of Kentucky. It is only an honest blow, but here at the base of such sounding boards, in the neck of rock, the end of the world, it would seem, is nigh. Wakeful, we follow the passing of a steamer, the shriek of her whistle magnified with wind against the cliff, broken and thrown down about us as fragments spin from a lightning crash, numbing our ears so that they seem full of soft mud and we cannot hear. Her lights in the rain are bright but have no steady contour. Her wake adds to the surf pulled up on the bank, kicking and fussing and wiping its foam.

Morning comes yellow and innocent, panting a little but playfully calm. Since we are never sure that on a next night we may not lie in weeds ill-fed and wet, we have no thought of pushing off. For a day of long hours we lie on pallets writing, sleeping, rising on an elbow to watch a steamer. From where I lie I can see my companions walking under the rock. Neither, I think, would lay great claim to difference from his fellows, yet against the wet wall swollen with humps of moss, hairy with columbine and spiral of young fronds, they look extraordinary. Their eyes and naked pink, their easy moving and halting, have in them something of the startling ardor of fawns, moist-nosed, ears erect.

And from where I lie, by crawling a little on my stomach, very still, I can see, and for once have my fill of seeing, herons. They walk close at hand on a finger of gravel that juts from the bank. They have the awkwardness of too much grace got out of hand, with the wobble and waver and quivering "feel" of springs unwound. Angular a-foot, with a little scoop of wing and a backward hop they can rise with unimaginable ease, and, having their way with gravity, take their time in coming down. They are young, but somehow nevertheless decrepit. At the base of their beak is a fuzz like bread-mould. And they seem also under-sexed; the females elderly virgins, the males too acquiescent.

Our last move on the Ohio brings us to Shawneetown. It is visible first as a darker condensation in the line of horizon, then recognizably a profile more and more distinct until, like all towns viewed from a distance (but particularly over water), it seems a finite thing, exquisitely circumscribed, having assumed ineluctably its present shape. Though its lines have been assembled at random, answering the needs of individuals, not responding to the will of one designer, it looks to be carved from one piece, like the bibelots chiselled in their spare time by mechanics (who had wished to be sculptors) from a sole morsel of wood or ivory.

Shawneetown gathered about the cabin of an original settler in the years after 1806. Men were attracted first by neighboring salines. But the long-legged West in those days shot up fast. With a mail route, a newspaper, a land office, with churches and with banks (that were built like Greek temples), the town before long was a nucleus for the whole countryside, a political, social, and commercial center. Rapturously sure of the future, its citizens seemed wise in refusing a loan of one thousand dollars to the village of Chicago, which was "too far from Shawneetown ever to amount to anything."

## The Ohio and the Cumberland

There are towns which have kept steadily, while all about them changed, a flavor of old times. Shawneetown is one of those. Its architecture, its street scene, its steps, its window panes, its columns and door lights all are dated 1820–40. There is no escaping it. You read it as an animal reads wind. It is turned on you like a hose. A poster announcing the election of Jackson would not be greatly out of place. Gentlemen in beaver hats and trousers strapped beneath the arch would seem to be moving among their own. At the corner a rider might rear his mount and fire and call some news.

Shawnee lies behind huge levees which, when the time comes, do no good. Seventy-odd feet above low-water mark the Ohio rolls into stand eight feet deep in the stores. Steamboats have navigated the streets with only a little extra trouble to the pilot. No man in his senses would have built the town so in the first, but, once here, its cantankerous refusal to be flooded out has got it affection and admiration. A modern Shawneetown is being constructed inland out of the way of the river, leaving the old town with a sort of skeleton staff as a monument to pioneer times. But there are folk who refuse to go. On the waterfront a man tells me of a friend who recently killed himself, chiefly because he was upset by this removal.

"Shawnee's always ben hyar," the man says. "Hit's our life. Hit ought t'stay. Nothin' else ain't natural."

Trying to console him (though I secretly agree), I point out that the annual flood *is* a danger and a bother.

"But ye got t'expect that," he explains patiently. "That thar's the way the river is."

## Where the Rivers Meet

And he adds what could not be wrung out of him if he were not stirred to the marrow: "I love hit jest the way hit is."

While my companions are repeating my stroll about town, I return to the levee, waiting for them in a floating establishment which occupies two flat boats lashed together. The one nearest shore is a lunch counter and soft-drink parlor, the other a fish market.

In the first I sit with a cold bottle of beer which I got by rapping on the table, calling thus from the fish next door a tattooed man who came wiping his hands on his trousers. On his chest was a purple cross with a scroll, "In Memory of Mother." I am alone with a girl who has a sticky "permanent," high heels, silk stockings and too much make-up. She requests that I put nickels in a machine which plays: "Oh, Mama! Daddy's got them Sweet Ellum Blues!" She listens staring off into space, tears rolling down her cheeks, grieved so that if I had not already uncovered I should take off my helmet.

Next door in the fish market there is brisk activity. Men naked to the waist, reptilian with tattooings that expand and contract with their movements, are receiving fish from small boats that approach in line from the river side. There is the grunt of the hoist and the quick fall and slide of the fish to the floor—gaping, gluey and thick of shoulder. "Cats" are affixed to hooks and skinned, the honey-and-ivory flesh emerging as in an anatomical drawing. "Buffalo" are beheaded and emptied: heaps of sliced bodies lie waiting for the ice. There is on all sides an

240

uninhibited carnivorousness; a thrusting and wading in scale and gut and blood; an unquestioning acceptance of what the Lord provides.

And as if the scene were to be set off with fine canniness by a detail foreign to it, there is a little Negro and a monkey.

The monkey escaped, some years back, from a side show; he attempted to swim the Ohio to Kentucky. One of the boys went after him in a boat when they " 'lowed he'd had 'bout enough." His fur is greenish brown, with pinkness of new mice about the ear and eye. His face is ancient as if, through successive re-incarnations of his corporeal self, the spirit had remained the same.

To the black pickaninny I give an ornage, oriole-colored in his fingers; and to the monkey a banana. With his mouth full, he shows his teeth and hisses at the boy, retreating from him, looking back over his shoulder, returning on all fours, blinking his withered lids, chattering and pointing to the boy but looking at me as if to warn me. The boy puts his wide mouth to the orange, walling his eyes. He and his compatriot the monkey are not friends.

When we have gone and Shawneetown once more is blotted out on the horizon, the Ohio goes violet and the sky turns black. Thunder unrolls as if immediately overhead. The river is rougher than we have seen it, rough in a way we have not ever seen it. There is no surface commotion. It moves slowly and powerfully, disturbed underneath in what the French call *vagues de fond*, depth waves. A body of it is pulled on and withdraws, the pivot of the movement far below. Surface water, unable to retreat so fast from the original impetus, hisses in bubbles forward down the flank of the backward flow. We too, of necessity, execute this manœuvre, and sensing that we have not full control, we head out to midstream away from shore.

At this moment, from a boat approaching behind, we see men making gestures; yelling something we cannot hear, over the wind, from the black circles of their mouths. They are fishermen we saw at the market in Shawnee, returning now to their shanties at the mouth of the Wabash. Thinking they need help, that possibly they are running out of gas, we turn charitably from our course to go see.

It is not they who need help. Angrily they urge us to stop, to get into the willows to tie up. A man, they say, might keep afloat in this with his motor—if it should fail they would not answer. They have no time to go looking for bodies.

Rain breaks upon the two craft moored among the trees. The air is pearl; the willows heave; the river rises in planes that tilt and spend their force against us.

Howling: "How far to the Wabash?" we hear no answer. But the fishermen point to what we had taken for a broad left bend of the Ohio, violet, stung and gray with rebounding rain.

It is there, the Wabash, the *Ouabache*, the eighteenth-century road to Michigan and Erie.

242

# VII

# THE WABASH

# The Wabash

NEW FRANCE was looked upon by its owners as a kind of game preserve. They wanted to keep it wild; to maintain their authority with scattered forts; to disturb friendly Indians as little as possible. They were more interested in taking furs than in founding villages. Yet to withstand the British, the hostile Indians and the Americans; to transfer pelts and articles of Indian trade, they were forced to keep life lines open from the Saint Lawrence to the Gulf.

The country lying between these points is huge even for us today with our mode of travel. Had there been means to lay roads through such a vastness it would still have been against the policy of the colonial government. Therefore the French routes were the watercourses, the portage paths and "traces" used by the Indians.

The Wabash River offered the shortest way from Quebec to the lower Mississippi and the Gulf. A man could enter the Miami (or Maumee) from Lake Erie and portage easily to the headwaters of the Wabash. He could enter the Ohio from the Wabash. Out of the Ohio he could go into the Mississippi, there to head north or south. Or he could go from the Ohio into the Tennessee and, with one portage into the Tombigbee, float down to Mobile.

The Wabash was a common highway for the Indians of the Old Northwest long before the coming of the whites. Its existence was probably known to the French in the first half of the seventeenth century. In 1699 D'Iberville, and after him Tissenet, brought colonists down that way to Louisiana. It was one of the great hopes of La Salle to keep the route open, to claim the regions south and west of Lake Erie.

But the French had inherited the hatred of the Iroquois. Shortly before the discovery of the country by the French the Iroquois had destroyed the Erie Indians inhabiting land south of the Lakes. There was still danger of their raids. Therefore the earliest expeditions from the Saint Lawrence settlements followed the course of the Ottawa River, portaging to Lake Nipissing and Georgian Bay to reach the Fox and the Mississippi. As the center of French interests moved down the basin of the Mississippi this route was used less frequently than the portages at the south end of Lake Michigan—from the Chicago, the Saint Joseph and the Kankakee into the Illinois.

However, at the beginning of the eighteenth century, differences between the French and the Foxes west of Lake Michigan checked activities in that direction. The French, forced no less to maintain a southern route, decided to fight it out along the shortest line. In 1701 they built Fort Ponchartrain (Detroit). They encouraged the friendly Miamis to settle at the headwaters of the Wabash as a buffer against the Iroquois. Still farther eastward they planted the Wyandots, the Shawanese and Delawares. The Wabash then became the principal southern route, the last of the great French portage ways.

After the French and Indian War the Wabash served as a path for British military excursions between Detroit and Vincennes. When it passed under the jurisdiction of the United States in 1783 the severing of political bonds connecting it with the Saint Lawrence deprived it of any significance as a highway. But the depression that followed the War of 1812 sent many people into the Northwest, into lands until then neglected for Kentucky and Tennessee. It was then that Tom Lincoln came up to Indiana, bringing Nancy and the chaps. It was then that Abe slept on dead leaves in the loft; then that he split wood and hunted squirrels like any border boy. This movement to the West gave rise to demands for highways. Products could be carted along the silent wood roads, but beyond a radius of a hundred miles they could not be marketed. A canal was built connecting the Wabash and the Maumee with Lake Erie. And the Wabash became a great highway once more. This time its traffic was no longer bound for New Orleans and Mobile. Goods went to New York through the Erie Canal. Loyalties of the people were turning East. Young Abe was learning the law.

Today the Wabash is fat and green and slow. Once or twice a year it swells and rages. Vincennes remembers then how Clark came overland from Kaskaskia; how his Virginians stood to their necks in the winter flood, hearing the sunrise gun of the post they meant to attack. The history of the Wabash is good to read. Clark and Tecumseh, Anthony Wayne and "Tippecanoe" keep one alert. But to travel the river now is another thing. It puts a man to sleep.

We left the Ohio in storm. We rode over the water of the Wabash where it releases itself as if in ease after great exasperation. Beyond its mouth, turning north into the flat back country, it deceives our hopes. It is like a canal. Since the great overflows of recent years many of the farms have been deserted. The banks look uninhabited. The afternoon sun is pitiless. We pound on and on. We climb upstream to a bend. We settle to the upstream pull, headed for another bend. It is so all day. Nothing happens. There is nothing to look at. Nothing to hear. Far upstream there is a tree still blazed with the mark of a broad axe blade. At that point you left the Wabash to portage to the Miami; to go to Detroit. You entered the Wabash there, coming in from Lake Erie, headed for New Orleans or Mobile. Voyagers, moving such distances, wanted the Wabash just as we see it—fat and wide and green and slow.

We should be very interested to know where the voyagers camped. It would be fine to get to shore; to lie out of the sun and take a nap. But must we choose between a swampy flat and a mud wall? Evening comes. The ground fog rises. Fish begin to leap. There is no choice.

# The Wabash

We nose into the first bank. It is soggy and it sucks off our moccasins. Beyond, where the ground is firm, it is covered with a tangle of wreckage left by floods. Bits of timber and cornstalks are lodged in the fork of trees above our heads. It is not worth our while to slap at one or two or three of so many mosquitoes. We eat some fruit and go to sleep, barricaded in the tent, in air heavy with insect spray.

Today there is no change. We might be viewing the same scene except that we note the flow of the water and the contrary direction of the boat. Having tried the lowland for camp we elect the alternative this time; a mud bank. It is high and perpendicular. It looks crumbly, as if it were "worked" by hundreds of earthworms. Scales of it fall, clouding the water. We lasso a stump at the top and one man pulls himself up hand over hand. The others, using the rope, send up the baggage. As the last man climbs the bank he remarks that we have forgotten the tools and the fuel can in the boat.

We clear a patch for the tent in the tall rank weeds and another for the fire. We sit talking as dusk falls. Mosquitoes are thick. The air is wet and hot. Bits of the bank keep dropping. We all agree that we are sick of the Wabash. We shall get to Vincennes as quickly as possible. We shall ship the boat by freight from there. We'll buy some clothes and take the train for home.

It is all settled. We pile into the tent, and because the mosquitoes are bad we tie the net down well, knotting the strings. As we drowse off a big piece of the bank gives way downstream.

Sometime between then and dawn we are wakened by a noise. We were all asleep, but each is sure he heard the sound as it began, as it grew toward the middle, and as it ended. There was a loud crack accompanied by a tremor in the earth. Then a long keen whining. Then the whip and splash of something hitting the water. We decide all this later. For the moment we do not talk. We know what it was. It was the big maple at the edge of the bank where we ate supper. No doubt it struck the boat as it fell. No doubt the rest of the bank will crumble now.

And we are tied in the tent, caught like kittens in a bag. In the dark we can find nothing to slash the net or cut the strings. My fingers begin to work of themselves at the knots. I am trembling like a coward, surprised at the last moment that he is going to be brave. The ground is shaking to be sure. One would say a locomotive was going by. The tent will collapse and carry us into the river. It may happen now. Or now. But it has not happened yet. A man falling from the top of a building might talk with himself so. The time between his pitch into space and his death on the pavement might seem infinitely divisible.

Once free of the netting we see that the tent is safe. A cave-in has occurred, but it is eating the bank on the downstream side of us. Moreover, now we are loose we do not think of the tent. What of the boat?

It is still there. When we have made a light we can see it floating belly up like a dead fish. It lies in a circle of sticks and leaves and dry samara of maple. Whether its side is stove in or not I cannot tell. But the tools are gone, the shear pins, the crank rope, the can of fuel. I know that my summer is ending here and not at Vincennes.

. I am not sorry. I have done what I came to do. I can go home now and sleep like bees when the comb is full. I have spent months with squirrels and chipmunks that sat humped as they opened an acorn, their eye impassive over the busyness of their paws. I have shared paths with rabbits that crouched where light shone through the thin tips of their ears. I have lain on a rock to sun, so still that a dove came down near by. It lay on one side, thrusting out one starfish foot, closing the other in a chapped red fist, lifting a wing to let the cool wind under. I have hidden to watch a young fox stalking pigeons, creeping forward on his belly. When they flew he broke and ran, looking up, not seeing where he stepped, rapid in the shadow of the flying birds. The squirrel, the dove and the fox re-establish an old harmony in me. I wish I knew ocelots and seals as well.

And I have found a new man—or one so old I had forgotten him. He lives in fields, in barns, and in the hills. He rarely sees a newspaper. Therefore he has to live only the passion and doom that fall to him actually. He digests them thoroughly. He has plenty of time. But he does not live completely within himself, poulticing the boils of his subjectivity. He is constantly solicited from without. He must adjust himself to seasons, to weather and the phase of the moon. He must use his arms and legs. His five senses must be keen. He says to me: "Listen! I hyar a snake that's got a frog." Two hundred yards down the bank he finds a snake. And the snake has a frog.

I could not have found these men and animals if industry had spoiled the globe as I had feared. This was the most heartening of my discoveries: that mill towns fester in one spot while the earth is green around them. The prairies will not be tamed. The hills will not be blasted quite away. The rivers will remain as the first men knew them—the long-browed men whose pipes and spears are locked in caves behind stalagmites. They will reflect our stars. They will mirror our bridges. They will be swift until the last ice.